W9-BZD-185

WITHDRAWN

SEVEN TIMES SMARTER

SEVEN TIMES SMARTER

50 Activities, Games, and Projects to Develop the Seven Intelligences of Your Child

LAUREL SCHMIDT

THREE RIVERS PRESS • NEW YORK

Published by Three Rivers Press, New York, New York.
Member of the Crown Publishing Group.

Random House, Inc. New York, Toronto, London, Sydney, Auckland
www.randomhouse.com

THREE RIVERS PRESS is a registered trademark and the
Three Rivers Press colophon is a trademark of Random House, Inc.

Printed in the United States of America

Design by Barbara Sturman

Library of Congress Cataloging-in-Publication Data
Schmidt, Laurel.
Seven times smarter: 50 activities, games, and projects to develop the
seven intelligences of your child / by Laurel Schmidt.
1. Child development.   2. Multiple intelligences.
3. Cognition in children.   I. Title.
HQ772.S337 2001
305.231—dc21   00-034418

ISBN 0-609-80509-6

10 9 8 7 6 5 4 3 2 1

First Edition

To my parents,
who gave me the armor of a happy childhood.

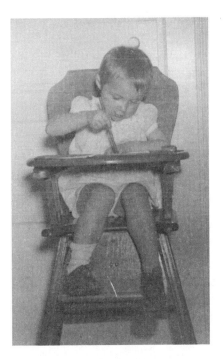

Acknowledgments

Good books, like good children, are collaborative efforts. This is particularly true in the case of *Seven Times Smarter*. Three generations contributed their wisdom and liveliness to its creation. First, I want to thank my parents, Robert and Dorothy, for their boundless love and inspiration. My siblings, Sheryl, Bob, Richard, and David, companions in this adventure called life. My dear friends and colleagues, Karen Boiko, Christina Cocek, Danny Miller, Pat Lem, Anne Brown, Bill Himelright, and Marolyn Freedman, who cheer me by their very existence. My mentors, Paul Heckman and John Shambra. My children, Thalia and Anthony, who are magnificent testimonies to the power of hands-on learning. Thanks to my editor, bright, insightful Sarah Silbert. To all my students who taught me more than I could ever teach them. And finally, to my dear husband, Durnford King, a wonderful writer, who believes in me when I forget to believe in myself.

CONTENTS

Introduction xiii

ONE: WHAT IS SMART?

A Word about Multiple Intelligences and How Kids Learn 1

TWO: WHO AM I?

Getting Smarter about Family and Self 19

Keeping Secrets

Memory Tours

Are You My Cousin?

Ancestor Maps

THREE: JOYFUL NOISE

Getting Smarter through Movement and Sound 41

Shall We Dance?

Wood Construction

Big Band

Blockheads

FOUR: IMAGINATION INCORPORATED

Getting Smarter on Your Own 59

Little Leonardos

Inventions

Tower Power

Do-It-Yourself Sports

Boredom Brigade

FIVE: EXPLORING AND DISCOVERING

Getting Smarter with Odds and Ends 85

Junkyard Genius

Collections

Where in the World?

Yellow Pages

Kitchen Sink Chemistry

SIX: WORDSMITHS

Getting Smarter about Thinking and Writing 105

The Postman's Pal

Stiff Cuffs

Pencil Pals

Author! Author!

Top Secret

The Play's the Thing

SEVEN: FINGERSMITHS

Getting Smarter through Handmade Tasks 131
Puppets
Pulp Fiction
Threadneedle Street
Patterns

EIGHT: BOOKWORMS

Getting Smarter in the World of Words 149
One More Story, Please!
Read All about It
Getting an Earful
A Library Card

NINE: RAINY DAYS AND SUNDAYS

Getting Smarter around the House 169
Potluck
Heart and Hand
Board Games
P.O. Box Scavengers
A Room of One's Own

TEN: THE EYE OF THE BEHOLDER

Getting Smarter through Art 195
No-Mess Art
Through the Lens
Look but Don't Touch
Secret Worlds
Soft Sculpture

ELEVEN: YOUR OWN BACKYARD

Getting Smarter Out of Doors 219
Just Add Water
Nature Watch
Hanging Gardens
Permanent Pleasures

TWELVE: THE WORLD BEYOND

Getting Smarter in Your Community 241
The Big Giveaway
Order in the Court and Other Public Meetings
Improve Yourself, Improve Your Community
Hometown Tourist

Index 257

INTRODUCTION

I've often said that my father's tombstone should read, "I'll be damned!" I must have heard that joyful outburst a thousand times, whenever he stumbled across a new idea or figured out how a strange building held itself up. It seemed he was always making discoveries and sharing them with my sister, three brothers, and me.

Dad was curious about everything. A self-educated man, in love with learning, he intuitively furnished our world with everything we needed to flourish. Years before Howard Gardner ever thought of his theory of multiple intelligences, my dad had discovered all there was to know about how to grow smart kids.

Our desks were overflowing with pencils, rulers, and stacks of recycled paper that we'd cut and staple into tiny books, turning the bedroom into a small press. The garage was another favorite work space. It had the cool dark smell of sawdust and motor oil, and just inside the door was a miniature workbench with tools that fit perfectly in our pint-size hands. Outside, a garden plot waited for us each summer. We were successful with carrots and lettuce, never with corn. While weeding, my father taught us the Latin names of the plants, how to prune a rosebush—and never to eat castor beans.

On winter nights he delighted us with treasure hunts, and if the evening was perfect it ended with five kids and a book tumbled together in his huge chair, mesmerized by the sounds of *Brighty of the Grand Canyon,* *The Littlest Angel,* or *Paddle-to-the-Sea.* The rest of the world dropped away during those evenings in the turquoise chair.

So we learned in that natural way that kids do, first watching, then getting in the way, then imitating while my father gently fine-tuned our efforts. Not surprisingly, I emerged from childhood with a fistful of skills. I could paint and sew and design furniture. I knew the difference between Gothic and Romanesque buildings and that camellias like shade. Corn doesn't. I didn't need much to have a good time. Given the freedom to browse and rummage, I could entertain myself for hours creatively and productively. I saw my mind as a tool for creating and solving interesting problems.

But more important, I had internalized six powerful beliefs that enrich every waking hour of my adult life. Here they are:

- Curiosity is the best toy in the store.

- Problems are opportunities to feel smart.

- When in doubt, read.

- Expect adventures.

- The human parade is the most fascinating event in town, whether you're leading the band or warming a seat on the sidelines.

- A parent's love and genuine interest are the best armor against the challenges of life.

I also knew with unquestionable certainty that I wanted to teach. I studied a lot of theories about how kids learn, but my success as a teacher came down to a single, indisputable fact. The more life in my classroom felt like my childhood, the smarter my kids were. Over the years, I learned to spot intelligence at fifty paces and coax it out of kids convinced that they were dumb.

Now I'd like to share with you some of the lessons I learned during one precious childhood and twenty-three memorable years in the company of kids. *Seven Times Smarter* is a salute to my four siblings, without whom childhood would have been an odd and lonely endeavor. It's a celebration of every eccentric, difficult, and outrageously intelligent kid who graced my classroom over the years. Most important, it's a footlocker crammed with ideas for helping parents have smart kids who will grow up to be productive adults with a knack for happiness.

You're probably a lot like my mom and dad—already doing lots of the right things. And I'll bet there's a lot more that you've forgotten, including some wonderful pastimes from your own childhood. Like making your own skateboard or organizing your pets into a circus. You probably thought you were just having fun, but chances are you were also getting smarter. Now your kids can, too.

Maybe you grabbed this book because it's clear your kids are sharp and you're pulling your hair out wondering what to do next. Good news! Without signing them up for another class or giving up your Saturdays or buying one more educational toy, you can open a playground for your kids' minds. Welcome to *Seven Times Smarter*. You're going to have fun!

SEVEN TIMES SMARTER

ONE

WHAT IS SMART?

A Word about Multiple Intelligences

and How Kids Learn

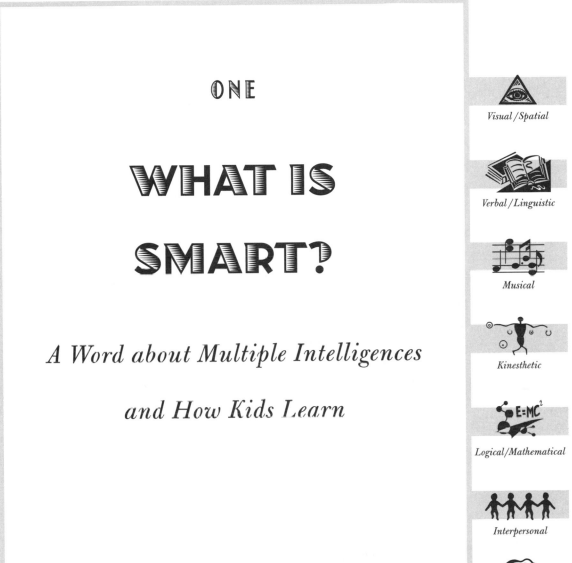

Visual /Spatial

Verbal /Linguistic

Musical

Kinesthetic

Logical/Mathematical

Interpersonal

Intrapersonal

Have you ever caught a glimpse of your kid as you peeked in his bedroom door and wondered, "What's he doing? He looks so weird!" Air-dancing to a commercial jingle, using the bed as a trampoline, or talking to three people who aren't in the room.

Did you think:

a. What the hell?
b. We need to see a shrink.
c. This kid is so smart!
d. All of the above.

The best answer is *c.* That's right. Many of the puzzling things that kids do are actually signs of intelligent life.

Smart kids:

- Repeat lyrics, poems, jokes, and stories word for word

- Whistle, hum, sing jingles, gurgle, gargle, babble

- Tap fingers, sticks, or toys rhythmically on a surface

- Draw on the bathroom mirror in the steam

- Take toys apart

- Make collections

- Create and entertain imaginary friends

- Make up games with special rules

- Skid or sock-dance on the kitchen floor

- Perform tricks on bikes, skates, or skateboards

- Prowl the radio dial, prospecting for diversions

- Build with blocks or other objects and knock them down

- Ask why and how things work

- Mimic the sounds of animals, machines, or unusual voices

- Rearrange and redecorate their environment

- Want to hear the same story over and over

- Make up dances to music on the radio, TV, or CDs

- Mix potions—sugar water or soapsuds whipped into a froth

- Befriend and care for younger children and animals

You probably have dozens of these "smart" pictures of your kids, but you might be thinking, "Who knew? I thought he was being a pain!" Researchers are discovering that many of those curious behaviors are clues to the special ways that kids are smart. If you learn to recognize the clues, you can help them get even smarter.

WHAT ARE THE SEVEN INTELLIGENCES?

What comes to mind when you hear the word *intelligent?* Be honest. Geek? Brain? Nerd? Do you picture a guy with glasses who can split an atom but can't get a date? Or a bookish bore who corners party guests to share the latest on cybermassage? Does intelligence just mean *school smart?* Absolutely not. Your own experience tells you that there's much more to being smart than talent in the classroom.

For example, you probably know lots of successful adults who never made the dean's list. Maybe they were even dropouts, but now they're great at what they do. Like the mechanic who can diagnose your car's disease before the engine's cool. Or the therapist who saves a family from self-destructing. Or the tenor who brings tears to your eyes. These people are brilliant, too, no matter what their report cards said.

And history books are crammed with famous names that never made the honor roll. Isaac Newton, Leo Tolstoy, and Winston Churchill all failed at some point in school. Thomas Edison was dismissed by his teachers as too addled to learn anything. And Albert Einstein didn't read until he was seven—you'd have found him in the low group for sure. All these people went on to make major contributions in science, politics, or literature despite their poor performance in class.

So it shouldn't surprise us that there could be a whole bunch of intelligences that people use to succeed. That's exactly what Howard Gardner proposed in his theory of multiple intelligences. According to Gardner, intelligence isn't the single IQ number we were raised with, but a mosaic of abilities located in many different parts of your brain. These intelligences are interconnected but they also work independently. Perhaps most important, they aren't static or predetermined at birth. Like muscles, they can grow throughout your life if they're nurtured and strengthened. Meaning that in the right environment, people get smarter.

Gardner says that humans have at least seven distinct intelligences or ways of knowing. They include verbal/linguistic, visual/spatial, musical, kinesthetic, logical/mathematical, interpersonal, and intrapersonal intelligence. Simply put, we're word smart, picture smart, music smart, body smart, logic smart, people smart, and self smart. (Gardner recently suggested an eighth intelligence—naturalist.) Let's see what these intelligences look like in kids.

VISUAL/SPATIAL INTELLIGENCE

People with a high degree of visual and spatial intelligence seem to have eyes "on steroids." They have a keen sense of observation and the ability to think in pictures. They can create masterpieces or find solutions to problems in the physical world, often without lifting a finger. The chess champ Boris Spassky, the crossword master Will Short, Walt Disney, the artists Alexander Calder, Louise Nevelson, and Faith Ringgold, and the architect I. M. Pei are all superstars in the visual/spatial world.

Picture-smart kids like to play with blocks; build with LEGOs or Erector sets; make forts with branches or boxes; create images with paint, clay, or computer programs. They like to design posters, arrange flowers, and rearrange furniture. Visual kids can find a face in a crowd. They're puzzle makers and picture hangers.

When they grow up they might be happy as architects, artists, automobile designers, animators, set designers, engineers, landscape gardeners, skywriters, computer graphics designers, plumbers, air traffic controllers, cartoonists, interior designers, museum curators, or photographers.

VERBAL/LINGUISTIC INTELLIGENCE

In our culture, linguistic intelligence is both common and coveted. We all talk. But very few of us can wield phrases like a magic wand or, if necessary, a sword. Verbal/linguistic intelligence is the generator for words and language. It includes sensitivity to the structure, meaning, and use of language, both written and spoken. Authors like Gertrude Stein, Langston Hughes,

Alex Haley, and Oscar Wilde and politicians like Barbara Jordan, Hubert H. Humphrey, and Benjamin Franklin were remarkable for their verbal intelligence.

Word-smart kids talk early and often. They collect new words and love to show off their vocabulary. They like jokes and tongue twisters. These children play story tapes over and over until they've memorized long passages from their favorite authors. Don't wait too long to introduce them to Shakespeare, Maya Angelou, and Douglas Adams.

A child who's linguistically smart might become a novelist, teacher, broadcaster, talk-radio host, advertising writer, tour guide, lawyer, librarian, public relations specialist, thesaurus designer, textbook editor, grant writer, speechwriter, interpreter, or comedian.

MUSICAL INTELLIGENCE

Musical intelligence combines the ability to recognize tonal patterns, pitch, melody, and rhythms with a sensitivity to the emotional or expressive aspects of sound and music. Megastars in this area of intelligence include Beethoven, the Beatles, Charlie Parker, Kathleen Battle, Frank Sinatra, and Yo-Yo Ma.

Kids who are music smart like to sing. They hum, change the lyrics in a familiar song, or repeat words in singsong patterns. Tapping, finger snapping, and head bobbing are clues to this strength. Musical intelligence can be seen in very young children. You've probably seen at least one diaper-clad dancer at a family gathering—apparently the only one who hears the beat.

If you nurture musical intelligence in children, they might pursue careers as composers, musicians, singers, choir directors, audio mixers for films or albums, disc jockeys, vocal coaches, music critics, speech pathologists, ethnomusicologists, or music therapists.

KINESTHETIC INTELLIGENCE

Just open the sports section of your newspaper or glance at the dance reviews to find out who scored big in kinesthetic intelligence. Kinesthetic intelligence fuels our ability to use the body skillfully or to express ideas and emotions through movement. It also includes the ability to handle objects deftly and make things. The work of Michael Jordan, Josephine Baker, Babe Ruth, Jesse Owens, Michelle Kwan, Merce Cunningham, and Marcel Marceau reflects exceptional strength in this intelligence.

Body-smart kids are movers and touchers. They know the world through their muscles. They enjoy building models, sewing, finger crocheting, learning sign language. They're great cheerleaders and they know when to stick or slide in baseball.

Kinesthetic kids might be drawn to careers as dancers, athletes, choreographers, potters, weavers, welders, auto mechanics, computer repair persons, carpenters, electricians, physical education teachers, actors, drama coaches, dance therapists, yoga teachers, laser technicians, stroke rehabilitation therapists, magicians, physical therapists, or airplane mechanics.

LOGICAL/MATHEMATICAL INTELLIGENCE

This is the intelligence that people typically associate with "brains." It governs inductive and deductive thinking, working with numbers and abstract patterns, and the ability to reason. Albert Einstein, George Washington Carver, Benjamin Banneker, Marie Curie, and Jacques Cousteau all displayed a well-developed sense of logic and math.

Logic-smart kids love word puzzles like the one about the farmer crossing the river with the chicken, the fox, and the bag of corn. Numbers are alive to them, like characters in a book. They relish mental math—estimating, measuring, calculating. Picture the main character in *Good*

Will Hunting and you'll get a glimpse of their world. While other kids are growing bread mold for the science fair, they're inventing a solar-powered homework machine. They speak computer fluently and never met a gadget they didn't like.

When kids with this strength grow up they might work as mathematicians, astronomers, inventors, traffic engineers, marine biologists, logicians, forensic scientists, epistemologists, urban planners, accountants, insurance adjusters, population or census consultants, ecologists, financial experts, stockbrokers, computer systems analysts, oceanographers, seismologists, astrophysicists, or water pollution specialists.

INTERPERSONAL INTELLIGENCE

This intelligence involves the gift of seeing things from the other person's point of view. It guides a person's ability to understand, work with, and communicate with people and maintain relationships. Martin Luther King Jr., Florence Nightingale, Harriet Tubman, Cesar Chavez, Eleanor Roosevelt, and Sigmund Freud were exceptional in understanding the feelings, motives, and thoughts of other people.

Kids who are people smart make and keep a wide variety of friends. They're the peacemakers on the playground and no birthday party would be complete without them. But they're not always the center of attention. They're good observers, too, perching on the sidelines but taking everything in. They like to read biographies to find out what makes other people tick.

Children with this quiet passion might become rabbis, genealogists, priests, teachers, salespeople, therapists, receptionists, social workers, child-care providers, mediators, advocates, convention managers, genetic counselors, hotline counselors, lobbyists, personnel managers, or negotiators.

INTRAPERSONAL INTELLIGENCE

People with strong intrapersonal intelligence are introspective *with results*. They develop self-knowledge, particularly a sensitivity to their own values, purposes, and feelings. This insight makes them independent, confident, goal-oriented, and self-disciplined. Emily Dickinson was a perfect example of a self-smart person. During a life of extreme seclusion she wrote almost fifteen hundred poems, one of which begins, "This is my letter to the World/ That never wrote to Me." Jane Goodall, a pioneer in observing chimpanzees, needed a lot of intrapersonal intelligence to create a life in the wilds of Africa and successfully share her findings with the world. So did Thoreau during his time on Walden Pond.

Kids who are self smart can work happily alone and contribute confidently to a group. They may begin keeping diaries when they're very young and do so all their lives or remember and record their dreams. Children with this strength are curious about their ancestors and may spend hours poring over family albums. As readers they're drawn to autobiographies, philosophy, and stories with a spiritual quality.

Their intrapersonal intelligence might lead them to careers as philosophers, researchers, archivists, theologians, animal behaviorists, anthropologists, archeologists, or medical ethicists.

THE SEVEN INTELLIGENCES
GO TO SCHOOL

With all these ways of being smart, why do so many kids feel dumb? One big reason is school, which can be a crushing experience for any kid, unless they have strong linguistic and mathematical intelligence. Many schools focus so intently on producing good readers and mathematicians that they routinely dismiss the other five intelligences, even though research shows that studying music or art helps kids improve in all their subjects.

A prime example of this bias is the way students with visual/spatial intelligence are dismissed. Parents wince, like they've been handed the consolation prize, if their child's teacher says, "She's very artistic." But visual intelligence can unlock reading, math, or science for many kids. Ignore it and you're asking them to navigate through school blindfolded.

Likewise, a child with extraordinary interpersonal intelligence may be dismissed as a social butterfly, when she should be encouraged to run for president of the student council. Intrapersonal intelligence is even less appreciated. The quiet child with a rich inner life may win a trip to the school psychologist's office or just get lost in the crowd.

Another problem is that far too many schools ask kids to sit still, keep quiet, and perform repetitive tasks in rooms devoid of art, music, and human comfort. In effect, to learn with their brains tied behind their backs. Or worse, in suspended animation. When kids don't respond well, the explanation usually involves some deficiency in the child, the parents, or both. You'll hear: "He's not trying." "There's no support at home." "She can't focus." "Maybe there's a learning disability." But just for a moment, imagine yourself in that environment, six hours a day, five days a week. How well would you perform?

In *Growing Up inside the Sanctuary of My Imagination,* the award-winning writer and artist Nicholasa Mohr recalls her struggle in school. A bright child, her bilingual outbursts regularly earned her a seat in the corner.

I would sit on a chair facing the wall, looking for discolorations in the paint, a crack in the plaster, or shadows on the surface. In this way I used my eyes and imagination to adjust these imperfections by making them take on other visual forms. On that wall I remember a variety of scenes, trees and waterfalls, part of a schooner sinking in the sea, and the profile of a horse. I was able to meditate upon these images and sit

under the waterfall or walk in the woods. Although I was still embar-
rassed and angry at the teacher, this game helped ease my punishment.
At the same time, I enjoyed sharpening my sense of fantasy.

I think kids know the ways that they're smart and they struggle to give us clues, seeking our validation and guidance. Yet day after day we damage them by failing to notice and respond. Sometimes we're blinded by our hopes and fears—"He has to do well on his SATs." Sometimes we don't recognize intelligence when we see it—"Oh, yeah, she's been drawing like that since she was two. It's good, huh?" When we overlook their gifts, kids feel confused and even ashamed. They don't just hide their talents—they bury them. Which means they may never get a chance to feel and act as smart as they are.

A WORD ON HOW KIDS LEARN

You may be thinking at this point, "Of course I want smart kids, but I don't know the first thing about teaching. Should I hire a seven intelligences tutor?" Happily, it's much easier than that. Learning is a natural human activity, especially for children. After decades of research about how children learn best, here's what we've discovered:

⇾ Children learn through play. It's the work of childhood.

⇾ Children learn through hands-on experiences. Seeing, touching, tasting, smelling are the strongest modes for early learning.

⇾ Children master communication by having conversations.

⇾ Children learn by trying to solve real problems.

11

→ Children find exploration and investigation intrinsically rewarding. The driving force is *"What if . . . ?"* and *"I wonder. . . ."*

So you can be your kids' best teacher simply by turning them loose in your basement, backyard, or garage. On their own they'll discover hundreds of ways to get smarter, with little prompting and no money changing hands. Using simple things like muffin tins, scrap wood, recycled cans, and old shoes, they can launch a learning festival that will run for years.

At first the sight of a kid pawing through your kitchen drawer, snatching up rubber bands and toothpicks for an "invention," may not strike you as brain work. But it is. If your kids paint their faces, don old hats, and serenade you standing on a kitchen chair, applaud. That's smart stuff. When they open a lemonade stand, teach their dog to fetch, or master the harmonica, they're doing mental aerobics. And the more they do it, the smarter they get.

FIRST STEPS TOWARD
GETTING SMARTER

When kids begin to explore their intelligences, they experiment and make mistakes. First drawings, poems, or dances are rarely masterpieces but with time and practice talent blooms. Except if there's a critical sibling hovering nearby, waiting to pounce—"You look really stupid when you do those handstands!" Even a casual remark by a well-meaning grandma—"Why did you make the sky green, honey?"—can cause a child to shut down completely.

So be a supporter. Celebrate your child's accomplishments. Applaud risk taking even when it results in failure. Compliment kids in front of siblings and significant adults. Put Post-its on the bathroom mirror that say, "I think you're a great goalie." Hang their paintings on the front door for Dad or Mom to admire as soon as he or she gets home. Call Grandpa when they get a home run or master "Chopsticks" on the piano. Words of praise are free but priceless. Don't skimp.

Orville Wright, master of the air, recalled the importance of having a cheering section when he and Wilbur were kids.

> *We were lucky to grow up in an environment where there was always much encouragement to children to pursue intellectual interests, to investigate whatever aroused curiosity. In a different kind of environment, our curiosity might have been nipped long before it could have borne fruit.*

Remember, you're the most powerful force in shaping your child's self-image. If you delight in your children, they feel loved. When you're fascinated by their projects, you confirm their value. Praise their intelligence and you bolster them against the negative reviews of the world.

WHAT ELSE CAN YOU DO TO HELP?

Once your kids get hooked on collecting, composing, or building, they may not want you around. Don't feel bad. Just step back and enjoy the break because it won't be long before they burst in and drag you outside to witness their latest miracle. There are rules for responding to miracles. Follow them.

⇛ Be a good listener.
When your kids talk about their projects or inventions, behave as you would with an adult friend. Don't repeat what they say (echo). Don't turn their statements into questions: "You built a house?" Just listen and respond with genuine curiosity. And smile while you listen. A frown, even

13

an unconscious one, can spell disaster for a project. Kids watch like hawks for signs of approval. Give until it hurts.

⇥ Ask good questions:

What made you think that?
What else could you do?
How did you figure that out?
What part do you like best?
How did you get that idea?

⇥ Do nothing for kids that they can do for themselves.
Don't finish their models, solve their engineering problems, or tell them how their poems should end. Leave it up to them, even if you have to sit on your hands and bite your tongue.

⇥ Avoid criticism.
Encourage kids to judge their own work. Reinforce their conclusions instead of giving your own critique. When you look at their painting and say, "Why don't you make the horse brown?" you may notice that your child's interest falters. She may even abandon her work altogether because she was going to paint a blue horse. Now she has to decide whose idea is better, yours or hers. The conflict may be too much to handle, so she quits.

⇥ Be patient.
Leonardo da Vinci used to sit motionless and stare at his paintings for hours. He'd paint furiously one day, without eating or drinking, then days would pass without a single stroke of work. It may take weeks or months for a kid to complete a project, read a book, or finish a work of art. Projects may evolve, languish, or be destroyed. But habits of mind are continually developing, sometimes with little physical evidence.

↦   Be a good watcher.

When kids really tap into their intelligence, you'll see the signs. They're excited. Their ideas grow and take up more space. They work longer and don't want to stop. They return to the activity over and over. Step back and enjoy the view.

↦   Be a good cheerleader.

Convey your delight in whole sentences, not just smiles and nods. Then they'll not only be smarter, they'll be happier. That's a gift only you can give.

WHAT'S IN IT FOR YOU?

If you're a typical parent you spend far less time with your kids than you'd like, unless you count carpooling, homework, and the hour you spend trying to coax them into bed. Who can blame exhausted parents for wanting to park their kids in front of the television, pop in a video, and head for a quiet corner of the house?

Unfortunately, this temporary solution leads to bigger problems— what I call the empty childhood phenomenon. This flourishes in kids who spend hours rooted in front of the TV—an average of forty hours per week for American children. When the remote is finally pried from their hands, what do they have to show for themselves? All the wrong stuff! According to researchers, kids who watch that much television suffer diminished cognitive ability and shortened attention spans. They're physically aggressive, mentally passive, and lack curiosity.

The dilemma is obvious. How can you be sure that their free time doesn't turn into the dead zone without feeling like a full-time camp counselor? *Seven Times Smarter* will help you. Think of it as a user's manual for young brains. A guide to creative independence for kids.

HOW TO USE *SEVEN TIMES SMARTER*

Perhaps you're worried that your kids are a lost cause—a team of surgeons couldn't get them off the couch. Don't give up on them. They just need a bit of a jump start.

First, thumb through the book and find some activities that appeal to *you*. That's very important. Maybe things you did as a child, or always wanted to do. How about something completely new that simulates one of your neglected intelligences? Choose something that requires no investment, like the cereal box city or disappearing paintings.

Starting with something you like will help you be patient with the inevitable mess. Having your living room turned into a tent camp may seem like a dumb way to get smart kids, unless you remember the delight of building your own quilted forts. As you thumb through the chapters, you'll see that each activity is coded with the symbols that show which intelligences will be stimulated if your child sets out in that direction. And most of the activities use low-cost, no-cost, and recycled materials.

Many of the activities in this book are taken from my own childhood. Others come from the lives of some remarkable adults who were very interesting children. For example, the Wright brothers, who had a habit of playing with toys until they were broken, then repairing them so that they were better than the originals. And Albert Einstein, an absentminded and messy child who had trouble tying his shoes but enjoyed looking for hours at the shape of a leaf and playing with his beloved metal construction set.

You'll meet Josephine Baker, Lewis Carroll, Rachel Carson, Gordon Parks, and Frank Lloyd Wright and see how their childhood pastimes blossomed into adult accomplishments. As you browse, you may be flooded with memories from your own childhood. Be sure to share them with your kids. That's how family histories are built.

The next step is the hardest. Turn off the television. And the Nintendo. And the computer. They're all valuable in moderation, but for many kids they've become a full-time job. It may be painful at first, but try to set a limit to the number of hours your children can be electronically entertained each week. They'll kick and scream at first, but be tough. Eventually, in the tubeless silence, they'll respond.

SEVEN TIMES SMARTER— ## AND THEN SOME

This book isn't just about boosting intelligence. It's not a recipe book for producing a third generation of engineers in your family. It is about helping you have multitalented kids who like themselves, greet the world with curiosity, and believe they have the power to shape a satisfying life.

In his autobiography, *Voices in the Mirror,* Gordon Parks, the acclaimed photojournalist, director, musician, novelist, and poet, gives us a glimpse of a life lived in seven dimensions:

> *The question frequently asked of me is why have I undertaken so many professions—photography, painting, writing, musical composition and film. I was just born with a need to explore every tool shop of my mind, with long searching and hard work. I became devoted to my restlessness. Today my imagination refuses to be confined to boredom. It stays hungry and I feed it with things that surround me.*

Remember, there's no reset button on childhood. That kid you adore could be missing out on an amazing life because he's too busy watching reruns of *Gilligan's Island.* But it doesn't have to be that way. Be a smart parent. Have a smart kid. Life's too short for reruns.

TWO

WHO AM I?

Getting Smarter about

Family and Self

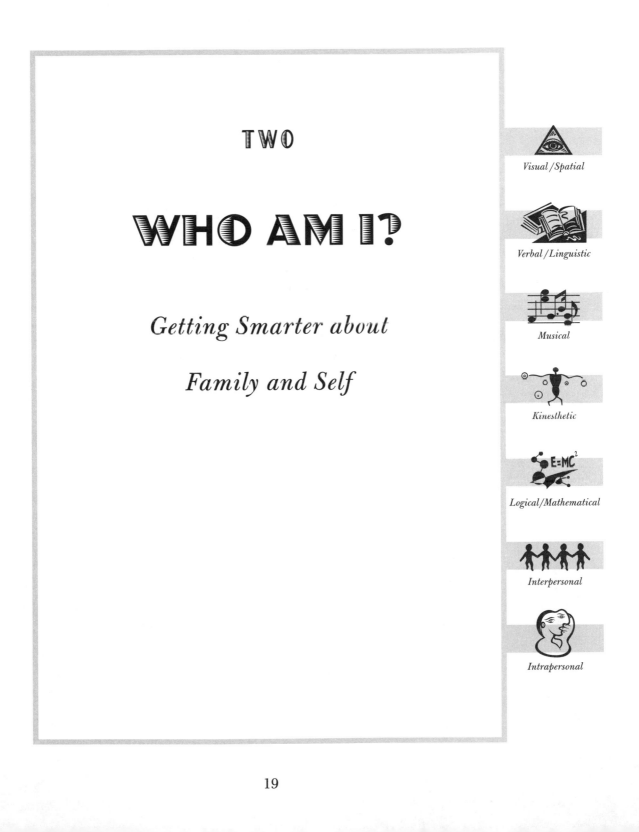

Visual / Spatial

Verbal / Linguistic

Musical

Kinesthetic

Logical / Mathematical

Interpersonal

Intrapersonal

KEEPING SECRETS

Do you ever stare at pictures of yourself when you were little and wonder what you were thinking and if you were happy? If you'd kept journals way back then, you'd know. Journals supply the subtitles for childhood photos. So help your kids chronicle who they're becoming with simple, colorful diaries and journals.

THE SCHOOL OF JOURNALISM

It's hard to overestimate the value of keeping journals. Every entry—scribbled, read, and reread—is an opportunity for mental, emotional, social, and artistic growth.

➡ Unloading in a journal helps kids get through the rough spots in life when they're feeling cranky, unloved, intolerant, or stupid but no one wants to listen. Knowing how to soothe painful feelings is an important function of intrapersonal intelligence, and kids who can do this develop resilience and the ability to move on.

⇥ Writing to express normal bouts of anger, hope, fear, or jealousy keeps emotions from getting buried too deep to reach. Using capital letters, exclamation points, and lots of adjectives is a way to yell without waking the neighbors.

⇥ A journal can be a room of one's own where kids go to explore their private thoughts and eccentricities without scrutiny or censorship.

⇥ A diary's a safe place to fantasize about fame, fortune, and true love without risking rejection. These fantasies can help kids dream their way to achievable goals.

⇥ Journals can be a laboratory for kids with strong linguistic intelligence. Emerging writers tinker with ideas that may grow into novels, short stories, poems, or autobiographics.

CALENDAR JOURNALS

A calendar is the easy way to introduce young kids to journaling. The daily boxes frame just a few words or a tiny drawing about the day. You can be the recorder at first and turn the job over as your child masters writing. This is a graphic way to strengthen sequential thinking, teach the days of the week, and look forward to upcoming events. At the end of the year, put the whole calendar in a box or envelope for safekeeping with your child's name and the date on the outside.

JUMP-START JOURNALS

The hardest part of writing is getting started. So jump-start the process with some teasers that help a young writer focus. Get a plain journal and write prompts or cues at the top of the pages. Here are some engaging sentence starters:

I wish . . .
My favorite . . .
I love it when . . .
I hate it when . . .
The best thing about . . .
When I grow up . . .
Tomorrow . . .
If only . . .

When it's time to write, kids just flip from page to page until they find a sentence to match their mood. Then watch the pencils fly.

DREAM CATCHERS

My Aunt Audrey has twenty-five years of journals filled with dreams she's recorded each morning before getting out of bed. If your kids like to talk about their dreams, put a dream catcher next to their beds with a good supply of colored pens and pencils. Encourage them to capture their nighttime images with sketches or phrases. Be sure to date the pages.

BEDTIME JOURNALS

Here's a simple way to build an attitude of gratitude in young minds and end each day on a positive note. Keep a notebook or journal next to the bed. Before hugging and kissing, take a minute to record what was good about the day. Young kids dictate to you, so it's efficient and very low stress. No spelling discussions this late at night, please! Your kids may want to make a sketch or you can do annotated drawings—they draw and you jot down captions or labels to round out the entry. Reflecting on the day's events helps kids increase intrapersonal intelligence, particularly the ability to identify and understand their own emotions. It also helps them recognize their strengths, so they can draw upon them in the morning.

RECIPE BOX JOURNALS

Get an old recipe box and fill it up with index cards in different colors. When kids are ready to write, they just pull out a card, write, and file it. Part of the fun and skill building comes as they decide how to organize their writing. All writers revisit their work, and these cards make it easy to edit, revise, make additions, or add illustrations. The cards can do double duty as story starters for homework writing assignments or recreational writing.

VACATION JOURNALS

A vacation journal helps young travelers observe and record their impressions while they're away from home. Suggest separate pages for the weather, sights, or people they meet. Or they can make daily entries with itineraries and highlights. Be sure to bring along tape so they can add clippings from the local newspaper, maps, brochures, postcards, even the paper placemat from a favorite restaurant. It's something to do when you're stuck in traffic or dinner is delayed. As souvenirs go, travel journals are much better than T-shirts and they last a lot longer.

OTHER WRITING MATERIALS

Here are some ideas for inexpensive journals or diaries: steno notebook, loose-leaf notebook, blank journal, or notepad. Half the fun of a diary is hiding it, so kids might want to keep it in a sturdy envelope, gift box, shoe box, old lunch pail, or cookie jar.

SNEAKING A PEEK: A BOOKSHELF OF OTHER KIDS' DIARIES

One of the challenges of keeping a journal or diary when you're young is that the same things happen day after day. Kids get frustrated when their journal entries look like they came out of a Xerox machine—*I went to school. Math class was terrible. Nora wouldn't sit with me at lunch because she's acting stuck-up again.* So they abandon the writing and slouch around, longing for excitement.

In retrospect, they might be having some adventures that would look great on a page. They just need to see a few good models of kids' diaries. A trip to the library is in order.

FICTIONAL DIARIES

There are hundreds of wonderful diaries, mostly in the fiction section, since very few kids sit still long enough to document their lives. Fictional journals are often lively and humorous, while giving readers a chance to witness someone else surviving familiar problems. A delightful example is *Heads or Tails: Stories from the Sixth Grade,* by Jack Gantos. It's perfect for kids who are nervous about middle school.

Many diaries have the added bonus of capturing another time and place, so kids witness the daily hardships of the Civil War or lumber along the Oregon Trail through mesmerizing first-person accounts. Try any of the following:

Diary of a Drummer Boy, by Marlene Brill, records the adventures of a boy who joins the Union army and ends up fighting in the Civil War.

Birdie's Lighthouse, by Deborah Hopkinson, is the diary of a ten-year-old in 1855 who lives with her family in a lighthouse on an island.

When Will This Cruel War Be Over? The Civil War Diary of Emma Simpson, by Barry Denenberg, records the life of a fourteen-year-old girl during the Civil War.

Winter of the Red Snow, by Kristiana Gregory, is the Revolutionary War diary of Abigail Stewart.

A Journey to the New World: The Diary of Remember Patience Whipple, by Kathryn Lasky, recounts the adventures of twelve-year-old Mem, traveling on the *Mayflower* in 1620 and living in Plymouth Colony.

Tchaikovsky Discovers America, by Esther Kalman, is the diary of an eleven-year-old who meets the composer on his trip to America in 1891.

Dreams in a Golden Country: The Diary of Zipporah Feldman, Jewish Immigrant Girl, by Kathryn Lasky.

The Ghost of Fossil Glen, by Cynthia DeFelice.

Across the Wide and Lonesome Prairie: The Oregon Trail Diary of Hattie Campbell, by Kristiana Gregory.

A Picture of Freedom: The Diary of Clotee, a Slave Girl, by Patricia C. McKissack.

I Thought My Soul Would Rise and Fly: Diary of Patsy, a Freed Girl, by Joyce Hansen.

THE REAL THING

Nonfiction journals connect readers with real kids who recorded their lives, often during times of war or great hardship. They're excellent for helping kids look at situations from another person's point of view. These literary

> *I started writing when I was about eight. Writing was always an obsession with me, quite simply something I had to do, as if I were an oyster and somebody forced a grain of sand into my shell—a grain of sand that I didn't know was there and didn't particularly welcome. Then a pearl started forming around the grain, and it irritated me, made me angry, tortured me sometimes. But the oyster can't help becoming obsessed with the pearl.*
>
> *Truman Capote*
>
> — GEORGE PLIMPTON

encounters help kids develop empathy, tolerance, and other valuable interpersonal skills that promote success in school and later in life. The classic book in this category is *Diary of a Young Girl,* by Anne Frank.

Others titles of interest:

Zlata's Diary: A Child's Life in Sarajevo, by Zlata Filipovic, is about living in war-torn Sarajevo.

Children in the Holocaust and World War II: Their Secret Diaries, edited by Laurel Holliday.

The Diary of Latoya Hunter: My First Year in Junior High, by Latoya Hunter.

MEMORY TOURS

As a child I bristled at the word *scrapbook.* My books held memories, and I bet yours did, too. Memory books help kids capture their childhood, piece by precious piece. They're visual history, autobiography, family archives, and calendar all rolled into one.

FAMILY RESEMBLANCE

Memory books nurture interpersonal intelligence by helping kids document their connection to others. Collecting evidence of their place in a family and a community makes kids feel secure. This visual web of support says, "Here's where I belong. I'm important to these people."

Collecting personal artifacts also appeals to children who favor their intrapersonal intelligence. They can look at the pictures and souvenirs for hours, studying the ways they've grown and changed. These trips down memory lane let kids tap into who they are and what they love.

Beyond their documentary and educational value, memory books can comfort kids struggling through a divorce. Having a book at each house helps co-custody kids feel connected to both families. Memory books also provide a vital link to parents in the hospital or away on business.

MEMORY BOOKS

Starting a memory book is as simple as loading a loose-leaf binder with lots of paper. Of course, you can dress it up with fancy paper, dividers, plastic sleeves to hold objects, and colored pens for labeling.

Kids can do-it-themselves just by stapling plain or colored paper together in book fashion. Or they can use a tablet of drawing paper that's already bound on one edge. For a cover with a personal touch, they can paste up a collage of pictures or photos.

Home improvement stores are eager to unload their outdated wallpaper books. These monsters provide enough album for a very busy childhood. Just cover the front with contact paper or cloth and presto! Instant archives! Kids can glue their treasures right onto the pages, then write captions or stencil words for headings.

Memory books are a wonderful springboard for developing linguistic intelligence. Kids are motivated to find just the right phrase to describe an old friend, a new pet, or their first two-wheeler. Kids also love to sit and talk about their memories. These nostalgic conversations strengthen recall skills, sequencing, and the ability to describe events accurately, with plenty of details.

DEDICATION PAGE

If you have a child who pores over old family pictures, no doubt you've found yourself trying to answer questions like *What was her name? What did she do? Where did he live? When was he born?* If only those long-gone relatives had left behind a letter of introduction for their curious descendants! Kids may warm to the idea of writing a letter to put in their memory book, including names, birth details, personal accomplishments, or family anecdotes.

UNBOOKS

A memory album doesn't have to look like a book. What about a folder with pockets for sorting and storing mementos? This format is particularly appealing to visual learners, who think in pictures. Get a long sturdy sheet of paper, fold up the bottom edge to make a pocket, then make vertical folds to create sections. Staple each pocket at the fold. Kids can sort photos, programs, letters, newspaper clippings, and invitations into labeled sections, categorizing and sequencing the big events and little changes in their lives. Tie a big ribbon around it to keep the treasures safe.

Kids can make albums with the commercial pocket folders that are used for business presentations and homework. Staple several together or run them through a three-hole punch and string them with yarn, raffia, or ribbon. Kids can add to this format almost endlessly.

MEMORY CALENDAR

Imagine parachuting back into your seventh year, complete with birthday cards, Brownie pins, and play dates with friends you've completely forgotten. A simple calendar can create this possibility for your child. Buy a hanging wall calendar. Each month attach souvenirs of the big events: school programs, ticket stubs, invitations, and photos. Then kids can write key words or draw little pictures in the boxes on special days. At the end of the year, put the whole calendar in a big envelope labeled with your child's name and the year. Or tie it up with ribbons and store it flat in a pizza box. These keepsake calendars could be the main attraction at your child's thirty-fifth birthday party.

SCRAP BOX

Some kids are kinesthetic learners. They absorb and remember information best when it arrives through their fingertips, so they need the freedom to touch, sort, and rearrange memorabilia. The last thing they want is to smash their memories under plastic. The best approach for these tactile collectors is a scrap box or memory box—a pizza box for large flat things, an old jewelry box with sections, a shoe box or sturdy gift box, decorated tins, picnic baskets, or an abandoned cookie jar. The more unique the better. And be sure it's stored on a low shelf so kids can dig in anytime they need a tidbit, snack, or five-course memory.

ARE YOU MY COUSIN?

Extended family can be a great emotional resource when kids are growing up. Unfortunately, geography often strains family ties. Phone bills can skyrocket. E-mail is faceless. So why not try video postcards—five to ten minutes of video footage that captures a glimpse of what's going on in your family? They're written and produced by your kids for cousins, grandparents, or friends who've moved away.

Now, if you've ever endured the boredom of a relative's home-movie festival, you might think the only thing worse would be home-movies by kids. So why encourage young videoists? Because these small-screen postcards can establish or strengthen family bonds, whether you're a thousand miles apart or just across the county line.

THINKING IN PICTURES

Making video postcards does more than just keep families in touch between holidays. It's like enrolling your kids in a writers' workshop. The minute they point and squint, they activate their visual intelligence to arrange settings, compose shots, and direct the action. Linguistic intelligence shapes the dialogue, characters, and story structure, so their brain has to work as hard as their eyes. In just five minutes of filming they may have to decide:

Who's my audience?
What do I want to say?
Who will talk first?
Funny or serious?
What will they be doing?
Real or imaginary?
Where will I shoot—inside or outside?
Do I narrate or just point the camera?

In answering these questions, kids are juggling the basic ingredients of moviemaking. Without realizing it, they're creating miniature essays, documentaries, biographies, or short stories that function as a lifeline between families and friends.

SCREENPLAYS

The possibilities for video postcards are unlimited. Most of the following suggestions give kids a chance to develop interpersonal and intrapersonal intelligence as they decide what aspects of themselves and their families they want to capture and share with friends and relatives.

Here's a starter list:

■ Shoot video postcards for friends and relatives just to keep in touch. Take the camera on picnics or to the Little League game, or set it up at the breakfast table and chat.

■ Holiday greetings can include singing, decorations, and thank-yous for gifts.

- Talking birthday or anniversary cards from your family to relatives celebrating far away.

- Baby announcements let big sisters and brothers introduce the newest member of the family.

- Film the new reader in the family showing off her skills and send it to Grandma and Grandpa.

- Film an older child reading a favorite story and send it to younger cousins.

- Take the camera to soccer games, scouting events, or school plays. Make video postcards for older relatives who can't travel easily.

- Capture your family tree on film at family gatherings. Be sure to include interviews, stories, and all the faces that make your family special.

SIMPLE VIDEO TECHNIQUES

Many parents think Kids + Cameras = Repair Bills. And the idea of watching jittery footage with a garbled sound track makes them want to pounce on the erase button. You can avoid some of these problems with a quick seminar for your camera-kid.

1. SAFETY FIRST
Put a neck strap on the camera and insist that kids use it. That eliminates the constant "Hold it tight! Don't drop it!" echoing in the background of their films.

2. STEADY HANDS
Some videos look like they've been shot from a pogo stick. If you don't want to serve Dramamine with your video postcards, teach kids

how to stop the camera from bobbing and lurching. If you don't have a tripod, a simple kitchen chair will do. They just sit backwards in the chair, lean the camera on the back of it, and shoot. Swiveling the camera produces a simple pan. If you have a swivel chair, that's even better.

3. SLOW PAN

Some videos look like they've been shot from a carousel. Kids can avoid this dizzying effect by following the rule of five. Count to five slowly—*One Mississippi, two Mississippi*—while panning. The whole pan should be at least five counts long. This lets viewers see details rather than a high-speed smear of light and color.

4. DIRECTOR'S CUT

Remind kids to turn off the camera if they need to talk to their subjects. Otherwise, the directions get mixed in with the story.

5. WHO'S WHO?

Don't forget about the credits. Encourage kids to write titles and credits on cardboard or colored paper. Prop the title pages against a chair or pin them on a wall. Steady the camera and shoot each one for at least five seconds.

RECYCLING CASSETTES

Encourage relatives to recycle the cassettes with messages of their own. You could reinvent the art of corresponding! If your kids show a flair for filming, check out the book *Great Careers for People Interested in Film, Video, and Photography* by David Rising.

ANCESTOR MAPS

Many of us don't discover an interest in our heritage—who we are and where we came from until it's too late. Our curiosity is piqued at a bar mitzvah or golden anniversary, but by then many precious family stories may have slipped away. So help your kids explore genealogy while the family tree is still in full bloom.

Making ancestor maps helps kids get acquainted with the people who came before them—aunts and uncles, grandparents and great-grandparents. Each map tells the unique story of where family members come from, the places they've lived, their accomplishments, and the role they played in their communities.

Doing family research appeals to older kids because it's like detective work. They prospect for clues, collect eye-witness accounts, and study photos. Eventually names and faces are knit together into the fabric of a family history.

TRACKING SKILLS

Like any good investigation, ancestor tracking involves a number of skills that exercise both linguistic and logical intelligence. While researching a grandmother or great-grandfather, kids will need to:

- Use an atlas to locate birthplaces

- Interview people in the family and take notes

- Record and organize information

- Sequence events and people (who-came-first)

Interpersonal and intrapersonal intelligence are stimulated when kids discover and diagram relationships, identify family traits, and look for themselves in others.

GETTING STARTED

Suggest to your kids that they talk to family members and go through family albums. See how many relatives they can list. Then they'll need to decide what else they need to know, such as *What was my grandmother's maiden name? Where did her family come from before they lived in Philadelphia?*

Buy a bunch of tourist postcards of the place where you live. You can get inexpensive ones at the dime store. Kids can send them to out-of-town relatives, telling them about the ancestor project. They can ask them to send pictures of themselves, their relatives, and their town to fill in some of the gaps. If your relatives don't want to part with old photos, the kids can ask for Xerox copies. Send along some of the questions and see if they know the answers or can point your kids toward someone else who might know.

Phone relatives, especially older ones who would enjoy talking to younger members of the family. Or make a plan to meet one afternoon and take along a tape recorder. They're full of stories if your kids just ask the right questions.

QUESTIONS KIDS CAN ASK

What is your whole name?
Were you named for someone?
What were your mom's and dad's names?

When and where were you born?

Where did you live when you were growing up?

What was school like when you were little?

What did you do during summer vacation?

What special traditions did you celebrate?

When and where did you get married?

What jobs did you have?

Who were your children?

OTHER SOURCES OF INFORMATION

Researching the family tree stimulates curiosity and develops persistence. Kids also hone social skills and make new friends as they troll for information. Suggest that they question relatives at family reunions and celebrations, and check photo albums, legal certificates, scrapbooks, and newspaper archives. Don't forget the historical society in your relatives' hometown.

PUTTING IT ALL TOGETHER

Once you've rounded up your relatives, past and present, your kids will want to organize their discoveries in a way that keeps them safe and is easy to share with others. Here are some interesting formats for telling family stories.

ANCESTOR STACKS

The ancestor stack is a series of round pages joined by flat ribbons. Each page is a miniature history of one member of your family. Spread out, they form a family tree. Folded on top of one another, they represent your family's history over time.

1. To start, kids need to cut eighteen circles out of heavy paper. They can be any size from silver dollar to saucer. You may need to adjust the number depending on your family structure. They'll need more if you want to include siblings, aunts, and uncles.

2. On one side of each circle, they put the picture, name, and birthdate of a family member. On the other side they can write interesting details about that person—birthplace, profession, special talents (painter, writer, pianist), nickname.

3. When you've identified all the key people in your family, arrange the circles in rows that form a pyramid or tree shape. The single circle at the top is for the child who's constructing this ancestor map. The family is laid out in succeeding rows below—parents, grandparents, great-grandparents. Label the center circle of each row to indicate the generation (parents, grandparents, etc.)

4. Attach the circles with short pieces of ribbon, following the diagram below.

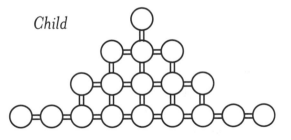

Child

5. Experiment to discover different ways to fold the stack.

6. Decorate a box or find a circular tin to hold the ancestor stack.

FAMILY POCKET MAP

The pocket map is a great format for kids who have a lot of information, pictures, and souvenirs about the people in their family. Each person has his or her own pocket and the whole thing folds up like an accordion. Kids can add to this map every time they learn something new about their relatives.

1. Take a long piece of sturdy paper, ten inches wide and as long as you want it. You can glue pieces together and add on to this as you go, but start with something at least thirty-six inches long.

2. Fold up three inches along the long edge to form a pocket.

3. Draw eight up-and-down lines four inches apart from one end to the other.

4. Fold along the lines like an accordion to create nine pockets. Staple or glue the edge of the end pockets so nothing will fall out.

5. Kids put their names on the center pocket, their parents' names on either side, and their grandparents' names next to them.

6. Pictures, cards, mementos, letters, and their own writings about family members are tucked in the appropriate pockets.

7. Fold the accordion map and tie it with ribbon or put it in an envelope, a tin, or a decorated box.

8. They can add to this for years.

SCRAPBOOK

A plain old scrapbook can be a good starting point for ancestor hunting. Kids can assign one page to each person they know and attach pictures, maps, letters, and written memories. This is a great time for visual and linguistic learners to add their own captions or drawings. Kids can also devote pages to family gatherings, vacations, or other events that bring family members together. How about a section for favorite family stories?

HELP FOR ANCESTOR HUNTERS

How-To Books

Netting Your Ancestors: Genealogical Research on the Internet, by Cyndi Howells. A recent book about using the Internet to trace your family history.

Do People Grow on a Family Tree? Genealogy for Kids and Other Beginners, by Ira Wolfman.

Discover It Yourself: Where Did You Get Those Eyes? by Kay Cooper.

The Great Ancestor Hunt: The Fun of Finding Out Who You Are, by Lila Perl.

Ancestor Hunting, by Lorraine Henriod.

Roots for Kids: A Genealogy Guide for Young People, by Susan Beller.

Who's Who in Your Family, by Jerold Beirin.

Fiction

Family Tree, by Katherine Ayres. An eleven-year old discovers her past while doing a family tree for a school assignment.

Homeplace, by Anne Shelby. A grandmother and grandchild trace their family history.

Seven Brave Women, by Betsy Hearne. A young girl recounts the exploits of her female ancestors, including a great-great-great-grandmother who came to America in a wooden boat.

Search for Shadowman, by Joan Nixon. A seventh-grader researches his family history for a class project, determined to solve the mystery of a relative accused of stealing the family fortune.

Be sure to share what you discover with other relatives. They'll appreciate your kids' hard work in digging up their roots. You might want to photocopy pages from a memory book to use as holiday cards or publish a short history of the family. It makes a wonderful gift.

THREE

JOYFUL NOISE

Getting Smarter through

Movement and Sound

Visual /Spatial

Verbal /Linguistic

Musical

Kinesthetic

Logical/Mathematical

Interpersonal

Intrapersonal

SHALL WE DANCE?

Dance is an ancient art form that's been used for religion, entertainment, healing, and communication. It can tell a story and convey emotions. Creative movement is as natural as breathing for kids. Go to any playground and you'll see budding Baryshnikovs reveling in the pure exploration of body, energy, and space.

Spontaneous choreography has all the benefits of going to the gym, without the membership fees or fighting for a parking space. The physical gains include strength, endurance, flexibility, balance, dexterity, coordination, expressiveness, and good reflexes. Plus, when you dance, you move. Move and you burn calories. No small accomplishment in a society where childhood obesity, high cholesterol, and heart disease are major health concerns.

THE MIND-BODY CONNECTION

If that's not enough to get you to roll up the rug, the mental gains are even more impressive than the muscle tone. Even the simplest experiments in movement require kids to invent, observe, and make decisions. They work by trial and error, using their kinesthetic intelligence to create and critique.

When kids dabble in choreography, especially with a partner or group, they use spatial intelligence to coordinate bodies in space and relate through gestures. In its most advanced form, dance taps into interpersonal and intrapersonal intelligence to communicate ideas and emotions.

Add to that the self-esteem that comes from performing and seeing the reaction of an audience. Josephine Baker recalled the sensation the first time she was on a real stage, filling in for an injured dancer: "It was as though I had swallowed a shot of gin. The whistles, the shouts, the bravos, the laughter, the hundreds of staring eyes were wonderfully exciting."

JOYFUL NOISE

I remember my first tap shoes—huge, armored, black patent leather. I graffitied the cement patio for weeks with my out-back-down-step-steps. It didn't matter that I wasn't very good. Shirley Temple, Fred Astaire, and I had something in common: noisy feet.

That's what kids like about tap dancing—the noise. Tapping is supremely kinesthetic. Intense sensations arrive through the joints and muscles, amplified with a range of sharp, scratchy sounds. It's easy to give your kids happy feet. Just hand them an old pair of shoes, some coins, and a tube of heavy-duty glue. That's it. Let them figure out how to arrange the coins on the soles. Wait for the glue to really dry, then turn them loose. Garage, basement, sidewalk, playground, even an old linoleum floor that can't get worse—they're all perfect places for the budding choreographer. With a radio, CD player, tape recorder, or their own voices for accompaniment, Broadway here they come.

MORE NOISE

If tap shoes don't appeal to you, there are other ways for kids to add percussive noise to their dancing without scarring the floor. Get some bells, like the jingle bells they sell at Christmas. Introduce kids to the art of needle and thread or just give them a bunch of safety pins. They attach the bells to socks, shirttails, gloves, or shorts and suddenly they have a costume that echoes their moves. Bells strung on elastic or ribbons can be tied to ankles and wrists, like Morris dancers who usher in the spring in New England villages or Native Americans at a powwow.

SCARF DANCING

This is a much quieter approach to movement that capitalizes on spatial intelligence. Scarf dancing lets kids see the lines and shapes their bodies make in space, like dragging sparklers through the darkness on the Fourth of July. This is important because essentially dancers are creating structures in space—like architecture. But each line disappears as it's drawn. Holding scarves, kids can see the arcs, spins, and abrupt changes of direction and put the whole structure of the dance together in their heads. By watching the scarf, they can critique and change their movements. Scarves can be tied to the end of sticks to extend the line even more. If you don't have any scarves or are in love with the ones you have, thrift stores always have boxes of them—very cheap.

DRESSING IT UP

There are lots of other ways to encourage kids to experiment with movement once they've got the basic idea. Get a box or old suitcase and dump in any of the following: peacock feathers to wave around, plastic swords, rattles, and, of course, hats, old clothes, and masks. A bottle of bubble liquid and a wand is another great way to define lines of movement. Bubbles create new dance ideas as kids jump, run, stretch, and swat at them.

WATCH YOURSELF!

In the art of the dance, the body is both the tool and the masterpiece at the same time. Dancers can't step back from the easel for a time to sit and stare like Leonardo da Vinci did. They have to watch themselves at work. That's why their studios are lined with mirrors. Maybe you have mirrored doors in your house that can serve this purpose. Or a patio or porch with large windows or sliding glass doors—when the light is right, they become mirrors. A videocam is another way for kids to study their choreography. They can tape, view, rewind, and tape again. Even their shadows on the sidewalk or a wall can give them feedback about their dancing.

CENTER STAGE

When my son, Anthony, was little, he loved to dance in the living room and watch his reflection in the sliding glass doors. Depending on her mood, his big sister, Thalia, would either play along on her cello or trip him because he was getting too much attention. End of concert! I'm not sure how the downstairs neighbors felt about our theatrical evenings, but these are some of our fondest memories.

So have some fun at your house, too. Any place can be a stage—patio, den, front porch, basement. It doesn't matter where. It just matters that you do it. And make a big deal of it. Pop some popcorn. Lower the lights. And clap like mad. It's way better than television.

LEARNING ABOUT OTHER DANCERS

Go to the library and check out the kids' biography section. Here are some titles to look for:

> *Letter to the World: The Life and Dances of Martha Graham,* by Trudy Garfunkel.

> *Agnes de Mille: Dancing off the Earth,* by Beverly Gherman.

> *Revelations: Alvin Ailey,* by Andrea Pinkney.

WOOD CONSTRUCTION

Somewhere in prehistory people began bending the forests to their own use. Branches woven into shelters. Trunks gouged out for boats. Planks lashed together for rafts, bridges, and fences. Wood is a basic material of civilization and woodworking is one of the oldest practical arts.

Kids love wood. The way the hammer leaves a trail of dimples across its smooth face and the sing of the saw. Building is visceral, creative, and deeply satisfying. And there's that element of instant gratification. How else can kids think of a toy and then have it, short of conning Mom into a trip to Toys "R" Us?

LESSONS FROM THE SAW AND SPLINTER

Wood construction used to be part of every first- and second-grade curriculum in the country. One teacher, thirty kids, and miles of soft white pine.

Kids learned about the harbor and built boats. As they studied the community, they built cars and fire trucks. A few schools still have brimming wood boxes and tool carts, but most construction programs have been consigned to the dustbin. Sadly, some powerful learning opportunities have been lost, especially for visual and kinesthetic learners.

When kids meet wood, their hands and minds are fully engaged. Even a simple crisscross airplane poses design questions. Where does the wing go? How long should it be? What about a tail? How many engines and propellers? Then the answers must be translated into wood. At that point, estimating and measuring are unavoidable. The actual sawing, hammering, gluing, and sanding all strengthen eye-hand coordination.

Construction calls for a variety of skills, but by the time kids are five or six, they're old enough to get started with adult supervision. There are kid-size tools at toy and hardware stores, and that's important because getting a good grip on a tool is the key to success.

If you're thinking that tools are too dangerous for your kids, keep them locked up and substitute wood glue. Kids can make dozens of imaginative projects from scrap wood and a bottle of glue. Just don't skip this important opportunity for your kids to learn.

Best of all, Mrs. Mason gave me time to play. I was even allowed to invite the neighborhood children into her basement where I constructed a theater. I asked Mrs. Mason for some old curtain material, nails and string. Boards set on bricks became the seats for the audience. I even had a costume, a fitted, tight-waisted dress of Mrs. Mason's and one of her big hats. I felt like a star as I grimaced, mimicked and danced to my heart's content, while my friends clapped and clapped.

Josephine

— JOSEPHINE BAKER

> *My family raised me to be completely useless as a do-it-yourselfer. I was not given a junior carpenter's kit as a little kid. And when I got a D double minus in woodshop in junior high, nobody at home seemed to mind.*
>
> *Chicago Days,*
>
> *Hoboken Nights*
>
> — DANIEL PINKWATER

RECYCLED RESOURCES

You can get your kids started in construction with little or no investment. Just simple tools and materials: hammer, saw, C-clamp, nails, and glue. Sandpaper, if you want to get fancy. That's it. Whatever you're missing can probably be found at a yard sale.

Wood scraps are the main item, but happily there are several sources of free wood. Call a picture framing shop or a furniture maker or restorer. Ask if you can have their scraps. You'll get lots of interesting shapes, colors, and bits with gold trim. A regular lumberyard is also a good source for plain wood scraps. Again, ask if you can come by regularly and collect their trimmings. There are also Dumpsters at construction sites, houses that are being renovated, and relatives' garages and woodpiles. Just put the word out that you're in the market for scraps and you'll be surprised at the sources that turn up.

CREATING A WORK SPACE

Working with tools can be lots of fun or frustrating and dangerous, depending on the work space. Trying to saw through a board on the sidewalk is almost impossible. Kids need a wood surface for hammering and a way to clamp lumber so it won't wiggle when they attack with a saw.

You can make a simple, safe workbench with discarded materials. Get a sturdy wooden box (old apple or orange crate, Coke box). Stand it on its end. Put a cinder block in the bottom to steady it. Add a shoe box, bucket, or basket to hold tools. Collect an assortment of jars or coffee cans to hold nails and screws of various sizes. That's it. Double or triple the work space by adding more boxes.

Here's another idea. If you have an old table stashed in the garage or yard, christen it as a workbench. If it's too high for your child, shorten the legs by sawing them off or plunging them into the ground. Or just use a sturdy box or cinder block for a step stool. Attach a clamp to the edge of the table and screw in a few hooks for hanging tools.

If you use a lightweight table, like a card table, put a cinder block on top of it to weight it down and stabilize it during sawing.

THE CREATOR'S CATALOG

Wood speaks to kids—girls as well as boys. They don't need much more motivation than the sight of a pile of wood and some tools. Their heads are full of images that they can translate into objects with very little help. All kinds of transportation—boats, trains, cars, trucks, rockets—become the starting point for city building and other imaginative games. Doll furniture, picture frames, treasure boxes, and animal sculptures can be painted, decorated, and given as gifts. Many kids like to build birdhouses and feeders which leads to bird-watching, nature hikes, and environmental awareness. See the section "Nature Watch" in chapter 11 for more ideas.

READING ABOUT WOODWORKING

Sable, by Karen Hesse. Tate loves to build furniture with her father
   and builds a fence by herself to keep a stray dog.

Go to the museum or look at books that show the work of Louise Nevelson, an American artist who constructs huge wall sculptures, almost like altars, out of scrap wood. Kids will love finding the chair legs, toilet seats, and croquet mallets in these somber black or gold constructions.

If your kids really get interested in building, watch *This Old House* or *New Yankee Workshop* so they can see grown-up builders at work.

BIG BAND

One of the greatest discoveries of infancy is the power to make noise. First there's the myriad of mouth sounds babies produce. Then when their grip improves, they graduate to smacking the table with anything in their reach. The sudden sharp rap of a spoon delights them. That's why they do it over and over until you want to scream.

Creating their own sounds intrigues kids of all ages. They drag sticks along fences, swat tree trunks, and delight in pounding almost any hollow object. The rip of Velcro shoe fasteners has been known to reach symphonic levels in primary classrooms, especially at rug time.

SMART SOUNDS

Those musical impulses can be channeled into simple experiments or a full-blown festival once kids learn to make their own instruments. Right now you're probably wondering why you'd deliberately encourage noise-making when most of your waking moments are spent trying to find peace and quiet.

Music making helps kids develop mentally and emotionally. When they attack a tin drum, harmonica, or tambourine, they're exploring the basic elements of music: melody, harmony, rhythm, and tone. Music taps into mathematical intelligence, particularly in its use of patterns. It can also help kids who may not be very verbal express intense emotions or moods.

Music making draws on kinesthetic intelligence. The sheer physicality of performing music and singing can act as a stimulant and relieve stress. So if your child gets mired in homework or gets hopelessly stuck on a book report, take a music break. Ten minutes with the maracas can refuel the brain for academic tasks.

RECYCLED ORCHESTRA

Long before kids ever play a note on their hand-made instruments, they'll be tuning up their mental strings to construct a variety of musical devices. Kids with good kinesthetic and mathematical intelligence will enjoy the challenge of transforming household objects into string and percussion instruments, even if they can't play a note. They'll need to measure, estimate, test, and adjust their materials to produce a variety of sounds. Imagination and persistence can turn a kitchen drawer into Symphony Hall.

Many of the following instruments can be made by four- or five-year-olds with a little assistance. Older kids can refine and decorate these instruments, then move on to composing.

> *Father was a great swapster and sooner or later brought home a cheap fiddle. I finally got big enough to tuck it under my chin and pick out a simple tune; and before I had finished school the fiddle was my chief source of musical delight. I reached the supreme stage of playing "The Irish Washerwoman" without knowing more than that the four strings were called D, G, A and E.*
>
> *Lifelong Boyhood*
>
> — LOYE MILLER

51

Oatmeal-box drum with wooden spoon drumsticks

Milk carton or bleach bottle struck with chopsticks

Coffee-can shaker with varying amounts of rice, sunflower seeds, nuts, rocks, pasta, or beans inside

Toilet paper tubes with objects inside and ends taped up

Two plastic or foam cups taped together at the lip with rice, beans, or dried peas inside

Two tea strainers taped together with marbles inside

Rubber bands around a box or stretched between two doorknobs

A scrub brush dragged over a piece of screen or the rough sole of a shoe

Keys on a shoestring

Bells sewn on old gloves

Shells strung on a heavy cord or ribbon

Kazoo, paper New Years' Eve whistle, or noisemaker

SODA-BOTTLE SYMPHONY

Gather eight large glass juice bottles or water glasses. Measure a small amount of water into the first container, perhaps four ounces. Then double that amount for the next. Increase each by four ounces, so that the final container has thirty-two ounces. The result is a scale that can be played by striking the bottles lightly. Some kids are very talented at playing water glasses by filling them part way with water, wetting a finger, and rubbing it on the rim until it sings.

KARAOKE

On their own these recycled instruments may not sound like the Boston Pops. That's why karaoke was invented. Encourage kids to play along with the radio, CDs, or their favorite tapes. They might want to tape-record their performances, play them back and try again.

ONE-MAN BAND

Challenge older kids to coordinate as many instruments as possible for a single performer, creating a one-man band like the device in *Mary Poppins*. This contraption is a marvel of engineering—strings, levers, springs, and pedals. It wouldn't be complete without a harmonica jutting out like the bumper on a Buick. For the harmonica enthusiast or just the curious, there are four publications available free from the Hohner company.

"How to Play the Harmonica"
"A History of the Harmonica"
"The Heart and Soul of the Harmonica"
"Some Famous Harmonica Players"

Write to:

M. Hohner, Inc.
Andrews Road
Hicksville, NY 11802

FINAL TOUCHES

Remind kids that any concert can be pumped up with the addition of hand, foot, and mouth sounds. They probably have a whole repertoire of hand sounds from smacking siblings, but encourage them to branch out. Stamping, tapping, clumping, shuffling, brushing, marching, and jumping in a variety of shoes can produce a veritable fiesta of sounds. And don't forget tongue clicking, clucking, whistling, oohing, aahing, and doo-wopping, just to name a few. This can become a real adventure as kids work arduously with their tongue, lips, teeth, cheeks, and vocal chords to produce designer sounds.

PERFORMANCES

As with dance, it's crucial that kids have a time to strike up the band. Anyplace can be a concert hall—patio, den, front porch, basement. It doesn't matter where. Just make sure that their creativity and effort take center stage. Warm up the videocam. Pop some popcorn. Sing along. And don't forget to invite the neighbors.

BLOCKHEADS

Do you remember playing with blocks? Holding your breath as an ambitious tower did a slow hula and collapsed? Or softly nudging a pillar with your finger, then enjoying the avalanche? Remember resting your face on the cool floor to peek through the door of a block house? I remember all that and more.

I loved block day at school. We built the police station, markets, and fire departments. Chalk marked the streets where traffic obediently paused for tiny stop signs. Boats sailed in the linoleum harbor. Then I changed schools and never saw blocks again until, as a young teacher, I walked into a kindergarten lined with block cupboards from end to end. The fragrance of the wood was so nostalgic that I was momentarily speechless.

Maybe I liked blocks because my dad was an architect. Looking at buildings was what we did. Frank Lloyd Wright loved blocks, too. His mom wanted him to be an architect, so she bought a set of Froebel blocks at the Philadelphia Centennial Exhibition in 1876. Nine-year-old Frank loved the polished maple cubes, rectangles, cylinders, pyramids, cones, and spheres. Later in his life Wright said he could still feel the maple-wood blocks in his fingers.

WHY BUILD?

Aside from the sheer pleasure of sprawling on the floor and playing Gulliver in their own world, building stimulates kids' spatial, kinesthetic, and logical intelligence. Building is first and foremost a way to explore space and geometry.

Some kids start with simple stacking, making visual patterns such as pyramids or towers. In the process they learn the rules of balance and gravity. If kids want to design a structure, they must solve a series of problems, including how to create a window or door in a solid wall, design an arch, or construct a pitched roof. All the while kids are testing their eye-hand coordination and fine motor skills.

LOW-COST BUILDING BLOCKS

If you're handy with a saw or know someone who is, you can make a wonderful set of blocks with about a dozen six-foot-long two-by-fours. Just cut them in a variety of lengths, give the kids some sandpaper to smooth off the edges, and you're in business. For columns, cut hefty dowels, about the diameter of a rolling pin, in various lengths. Be sure to cut at least two of each length to make the frames for doorways and gates. Even easier, you can ask the lumberyard to save the scraps from the saw table, and in time you'll have a very interesting building set. Wood blocks stack well in an old suitcase, which can slide under the bed between building projects.

> *Einstein was happy to play with Maya, but he was most content when absorbed in some puzzle or other. Like the boy Isaac Newton, he liked constructing models, his favourite toy being a building block set.*
>
> *Einstein: A Life in Science*
>
> — MICHAEL WHITE AND JOHN GRIBBIN

NO-COST BUILDING BLOCKS

You don't have to spend any money to have a block set that can grow and grow. It's already in your kitchen cupboards. Recycling most of the cardboard products in your pantry will create a fabulous building set.

Here are just a few possibilities: salt boxes, baking powder cans, spice boxes, oatmeal boxes, shoe boxes, cereal boxes taped shut for stability, Band-Aid boxes, liquor boxes, cornstarch boxes, cracker boxes, coffee cans, potato chip cylinders. If the lighter boxes tend to fall over, put a can of soup or tuna or a bar of soap in each to stabilize the structure. When kids are tired of building, just dump the containers in a large box or plastic garbage bag for storing.

RECYCLED CITIES

If kids want to do some city building, they can convert the cardboard boxes into hotels, restaurants, factories, or schools with just a little creativity. Glue paper on the boxes, then paint. Use pens or contact paper to suggest windows and doors. Letters cut from newspapers or magazines make signs and billboards.

City building challenges kids to consider urban planning issues that still puzzle adults. How wide should streets be? How tall is too tall? What about zoning? Do people want to live next to a fire station? What are the essential services in a city? This process ultimately leads kids to think about what makes a city livable and gives them a new appreciation for the built environment.

FIELD TRIPS

Visit a construction site in your neighborhood several times so kids can see a building go through the various stages from skeleton to finished structure. If you can, walk through a house that's just at the framing stage with no solid walls. See if kids can guess which room is which by the size, location, and plumbing.

BOOKS FOR BUILDERS

Browse both the art and architecture sections of the library. Look at books of fantasy drawings by M. C. Escher, especially the ones with elaborate staircases, domes, walls, and castles.

Enjoy all the books created by David Macaulay, including *Pyramid, City, Skyscraper,* and *Cathedral.* Through delicate line drawings and engaging narratives, Macaulay works from the ground up, demystifying complex structures and the people who built them.

And don't miss Stephen Biesty's "Incredible Cross-Sections" series. Through detailed drawings kids can learn what's inside a castle, a man-o'-war, the Empire State Building, an opera house, an ocean liner, and more. This really builds structural intelligence.

Two more stunning books are *Bridges* and *Skyscrapers* by Judith Dupre. Six inches wide and eighteen inches long, these shaped books capture the essence of these structures in beautiful black-and-white photos.

MENTORS

The American Institute of Architects (AIA) has local chapters that often sponsor education programs for young designers. Architects will meet with kids, give them an insider's view of the world of architecture, and encourage budding builders.

FOUR

IMAGINATION INCORPORATED

Getting Smarter on Your Own

Visual/Spatial

Verbal/Linguistic

Musical

Kinesthetic

Logical/Mathematical

Interpersonal

Intrapersonal

LITTLE LEONARDOS

I remember watching my father and brothers start dozens of models. There was the great poring over directions, the snapping and sorting of tiny gray bits, and the way one piece always disappeared, as if it were a sock on laundry day.

I recall paint bottles the size of chess pieces and brushes so thin that they bent under the weight of a single drop of color. So many nights with the kitchen table swathed in newspaper, but not so many finished models.

NOT QUITE MODEL BEHAVIOR

The problem with models for young children is that they're expected to replicate things that are often far too complicated for their fingers and minds. In an effort to help, parents come to the rescue, but the results can be disastrous. They lose their patience and take over. Every piece is repositioned before the glue dries. Frustration turns to threats—"I'm not buying one more model until you finish the last three you started." In desperation they complete the project while the kids watch TV. This "fun" activity often leaves children demeaned and parents discouraged.

UN-MODELS

Here's a slightly unorthodox approach to model making that's a more constructive way for kids to tinker with form and function. Rather than plowing through pages of fine-print directions, kids want to get their hands on the pieces right away. And that's exactly where the truly powerful learning starts. As they snatch up the tiny plastic bits, they're thinking: *I wonder how these parts fit together? What if . . . ?* At this point, logical, spatial, and kinesthetic intelligence have meshed to help kids puzzle their way from parts to whole. Observation and innovation are the rules of the road.

So throw away the directions and just let your kid go for it. Maybe he'll only use half the parts and the end-product will look like a motorized mailbox. So what? It'll require dozens of decisions and much more creativity than doggedly grinding through Steps 1–45. Keep your focus on the important question: What is your child learning? For a start, to analyze parts by shape and size, to discover how they fit together, to create a mental picture and give it physical form, to begin with one idea and transform it through imagination and experiments. Even if the final product looks nothing like the shiny picture on the package, it's a model of problem solving and creative design.

THE PARTS SHOP APPROACH

For younger model-makers, buy several simple models and mix them all together, like a parts shop. Now model making becomes an open-ended design project that's risk free. There's no right or wrong answer. No critique from adults. More important, the child-designer defines and invents something from scratch, which takes a whole lot more brainpower than simply putting Part A into Slot B with a vague longing to be finished.

> *I would sit among festoons and nibble dates and try to make a model man-o'-war, following the Instructions for Little Engineers, and produce what might be mistaken for a sea-going tramcar.*
>
> *A Child's Christmas in Wales*
>
> — DYLAN THOMAS

STARTING FROM SCRAP

Or forget about buying plastic models. Kids can make the best models out of scrap wood and junk. Gather up a bag of wood scraps, some small nails, a tack hammer, and a bottle of glue. If you want to get fancy, throw in a variety of upholstery tacks, beer bottle caps or pop-top rings, metal lids, wooden tongue depressors, toothpicks, strawberry baskets, cigar tubes, shoelaces, spools, cloth, and used tape dispensers.

With these materials kids can create airplanes, helicopters, cars and trucks, fire engines, and boats. A little paint, nail polish, or marking pen will add the finishing touches.

INVENTIONS

Inventors are magicians in reverse. They see what's missing and make it appear. Now you don't see it. Now you do. House too cold? Invent a stove. Having trouble reading? Bifocals. Perhaps you need a lightning rod or a clothespress? If you'd lived in colonial Philadelphia, all these wonders and more would have appeared thanks to your neighborhood inventor, Ben Franklin.

Inventors' minds are special in at least four ways. They're fluent, flexible, elaborate, and original. Which means that if you give them a problem, they'll come up with lots of relevant, detailed ideas that would never occur to the rest of us. Inventing is really creativity with a job description.

INVENTING INVENTORS

Kids are natural inventors. Why take the trash downstairs when a pulley-and-basket rig will do the dumping? Why abandon a warm bed to shut off the alarm clock if you can silence the pest with a long stick?

Here are some ways to encourage inventing:

⇢   Nurture young inventors by modeling curiosity. Puzzle out loud about ways to solve problems, and welcome their ideas. If you're always misplacing your keys, ask your kids to invent a way to keep track of them. If the bird sprays seeds on the floor beneath her cage, what can they suggest that will help?

⇢   Encourage divergent approaches to everyday situations. If your kids think of a better way to do dishes or make the bed, let them try it once, even if it involves using ropes and pulleys.

⇢   Show a genuine interest in your children's ideas and inventions. Ask questions but don't critique.

Sometimes inventing is just a mental sport. When my son, Anthony, was about six he spent half his carpool time inventing ways to make cars burglarproof using fingerprint or voice recognition. The rest of the time he listened to stories by Charles Dickens or Douglas Adams, memorizing long passages from both. Those were wonderful times.

THE INVENTOR'S CATALOG

At first glance the things kids invent may seem silly. But if you look closely, there's a lot of mental muscle behind their creations. Young inventors generally rely on logical and spatial intelligence. They manipulate ideas and objects in their heads, often running through a series of transformations until they hit upon a solution.

Sometimes their starting point is more like a daydream than a science project. They wonder how some object might be bent to their needs and then the mind prospects for solutions. Other kids use a more logical approach. The invention is their goal, so they work backwards from the vision to what it takes to produce it. In either case, kids who invent are able to handle long chains of reasoning, testing and modifying along the way until the lightbulb goes on.

Kids invent for the same reasons as adults: economy, efficiency and novelty. And, of course, a better mousetrap. Speaking of traps, here's a shortlist of things kids like to invent.

TRAPS

Usually designed for insects, pets, or wild animals (real or imagined) who trespass on your block. They're generally so harmless that even the most docile domestic pet can outwit or outrun the trapper, but be sure to check.

SECURITY PATROL

Kids use string, bells, hangers, marbles, buckets, and aluminum cans to devise burglar alarms, intruder detectors, and locks for diaries and other treasures.

HOLDERS

Anything that will allow them to have their hands free. An enterprising student invented a cocktail-party helper. It was a snack tray–cup holder that fitted snugly on the forearm with a padded cuff. You could eat, drink, and shake hands without losing an hors d'oeuvre.

LABOR-SAVING DEVICES

Anything that kids don't want to do is a perfect starting point for an invention. They'll spend hours devising a crane to pick up dirty clothes rather than take thirty seconds to bend over. Automatic door-closers, remote control toilet flushers, delivery systems for upstairs and down, and, of course, the mythic homework machine. One kid invented a sock-saver with a dozen large safety pins. He'd pin his socks together the moment they left his feet, and he never had to sort or search again. I'd call that a time-saver. On second thought, I'd call it a miracle.

TRAINING COURSES

Usually for animals but sometimes road-tested on younger siblings, these include tricks dogs don't want to learn, even if you give them great treats. Rodents and birds are sometimes cooperative and you may get an invitation to a pet show out of this one.

TRANSFORMED TOYS

If you resist the cry "I'm bored" and make kids responsible for their own entertainment, they'll frequently invent new uses for old toys. Several cardboard boxes lashed to a wagon become a mobile home that can be towed by a bike. Dolls become puppets with the help of some long sticks and a curtain.

> *About that time, I invented a burglar alarm, which was a very simple-minded thing: it was just a big battery and a bell connected with some wire. When the door to my room opened, it pushed the wire against the battery and closed the circuit, and the bell would go off.*
>
> *Surely You're Joking, Mr. Feynman*
>
> — Richard Feynman

Fantasy Inventions

I knew a group of kids who spent their summer building time machines. Refrigerator boxes were outfitted with maps, reading lights, tape recorders, and a full range of control mechanisms. These kids were gone for centuries in their own backyard.

Culinary Concoctions

Lots of kids are kitchen inventors. Food speaks to them. When their creative juices start to flow, you have a treat in store. They might concoct a new sandwich filling or cracker topping. Maybe olives in the macaroni and cheese? You'll know after a few sessions if they have a flare for food or just want to mess with spoons and bowls. If they like liquids, try the section "Just Add Water" in chapter 11. But if you seem to have a budding chef on your hands, turn to the "Potluck" section in chapter 9 for dozens of ideas.

READ ALL ABOUT IT

If you have a serious kid-inventor in your house, I suggest you get *The Kids' Invention Book,* by Arlene Erlbach. It profiles eleven inventors, ages eight to fourteen; describes the steps in inventing; and discusses patents, lawyers, contests, and clubs.

Check out *The Way Things Work* by David Macaulay to get up close and mechanical with dozens of machines and tools, all beautifully illustrated.

Don't miss these books about real-life inventors:

The Real McCoy: The Life of an African-American Inventor, by Wendy Towle.

The Picture History of Great Inventors, by Gillian Clements.

The Hidden Contributors: Black Scientists and Inventors in America, by Aaron Klein.

> *Inventors must be poets so that they may have imagination.*
> — Thomas Alva Edison

FICTION ABOUT INVENTING

Ugh, by Arthur Yorinks. This is the story of a man who invents the wheel and the bad reviews his invention receives.

The Gadget War, by Betsy Duffey, is the story of Kelly, a girl with a desk full of tools and head full of ideas for inventions, who wants to be a "Gadget Wiz."

Almost Famous, by David Getz, tells of a ten-year-old girl who wants to become a famous inventor so she can find a cure for her brother's heart condition.

Herbert Binns and the Flying Tricycle, by Caroline Castle.

The Trouble with Dad, by Babette Cole.

The Marvelous Inventions of Alvin Fernald, by Clifford Hicks.

The Mysterious Machine, by Glen Dines.

TOWER POWER

I'm not sure what's more fascinating about towers—the way they make a staircase to the sky or the fabulous view once you get there. I just know that people love them, especially kids.

Very young children instinctively pile blocks up just to see how high they'll go before a spectacular fall. What looks like child's play is the product of logical, spatial, and kinesthetic intelligence. Kids who build towers are thinking every step of the way, managing mass, stress, symmetry, balance, and ever present gravity. It's physics, engineering, and architecture all rolled into one graceful spire.

TOWERING INTELLIGENCE

Tower-builders strain their logic circuits with questions like *How tall? How slender? How large must the base be? What will send this jittery construction tumbling down?* Kids quickly discover the link between aesthetics and engineering when they pit their design against gravity. The more they master the laws of physics, the more creative they can be.

Tower building is a precision activity that tests judgment and impulse control. It draws on kinesthetic intelligence for eye-hand coordination, particularly the fine motor skills needed to place the final piece. To build towers, kids must plan and maintain their focus at every step, and these abilities promote success in many classroom activities.

You don't have to buy expensive kits to encourage tower building. Some of the best materials are cheap or free and conveniently located in your cupboards.

TOILET PAPER PINNACLES

With a couple of family-size packages of toilet paper, kids are in business. They can experiment without noise, damage, or mess. This is basic tower work—creating a foundation, providing support and stability, balancing by distributing weight. The product may be a chunky step-pyramid or a wobbly spiral, but it's good, clean fun.

TUPPERWARE TOWERS

Clean the kitchen floor, open the cupboards, and you've got the makings for a great morning or afternoon of building. Pull out the Tupperware, cottage cheese and yogurt cartons, water bottles, strawberry baskets, take-out containers, and nested plastic bowls. Tupperware towers can be held together with tape or just piled, pulled down, and piled again.

PLAYING-CARD COLUMNS

Building towers with cards is the domain of the kinesthetically brilliant. It's an exquisite exercise in fine motor skills and patience. Kids dabble in engineering as they test the stability of triangles, rectangles, and squares in their designs. It's traditional to use playing cards, but greeting cards, index cards, baseball cards, and business cards are all perfect materials for building these fragile structures. Just don't slam the door or sneeze.

STRAW STEEPLES

There are several approaches to these spidery structures. Kids can tape straws together or stick one end into another to make triangular or square units, then tape them into a tower.

TOOTHPICK TURRETS

Toothpicks are perfect for making delicate towers, bridges, and buildings. Hook them together like Tinkertoys using raisins, miniature marshmallows, gumdrops, peas, or little balls of clay or homemade play dough (see recipe, page 215) and you've got a construction set with endless possibilities. Eating along the way makes it even more fun.

NEWSPAPER SPIRES

These towers are made from newspaper rolled into stiff tubes, then stapled or taped together into a variety of structures. Take three or four sheets of newspaper and lay them on top of one another. Start at one corner and roll the paper diagonally to the opposite corner. Rolling around a pencil can help you get a tight, uniform tube. Cut the ends off with a scissors because they will be weak, then join the pieces together at the ends with staples or tape. Kids can prepare units such as squares or triangles, then attach them to make a tower. Triangles can also be used to make a geodesic dome. Industrious kids can make a dome big enough to crawl into, then cover it with a sheet or tarp to create a private play space.

STYROFOAM SKYSCRAPERS

The molded Styrofoam packing material that lines appliance boxes is perfect for building towers that have both height and mass. Unlike the delicate card or toothpick towers that demand cautious precision, these chunky towers involve large-muscle movements and the manipulation of irregular shapes to create a balanced whole.

Styrofoam is featherweight, indestructible, and quiet. Many pieces have odd-shaped openings, so they can be notched together or easily attached with tape, wire, or toothpicks or just piled up until they teeter and collapse. Check behind stores selling appliances or any type of electronic equipment to find a surplus of Styrofoam blocks. Between building sessions, store them in large garbage bags.

BRIDGES

Think of a bridge as a tower on its side. Instead of sway, designers are fighting sag. Many of the materials discussed above—especially the toothpicks, straws, and newspapers   can be recycled to build bridges.

DO-IT-YOURSELF SPORTS

I'm no athlete, so I could be wrong, but it appears to me that when athletic adults lay down their burdens and surrender to leisure, they're inexplicably drawn to activities that require extreme exertion, tedious repetition, or levels of pain that the rest of us try to avoid. Call me crazy, but kids seem to be better at having fun and somehow they never get tired.

That's why they need lots of options when they go out to play—and I don't mean a lot of expensive equipment. Instead, teach them to create their own games, tailored to their interests and abilities. Inventing games can breathe new life into old sports equipment and rescue an afternoon drifting dangerously toward boredomania.

STRATEGIES AND TACTICS IN THE AD-HOCKEY WORLD

Athletes, whether Little Leaguers or pros, think on their feet. They display their kinesthetic intelligence through balance, dexterity, coordination, and reflexes that make other people stand up and cheer. When kids move from playing games to creating them, they have to throw a few more intelligences into the lineup because inventing new games takes mental muscles.

First, there has to be a goal for the game, with clear rules, strategies, and a way to keep score. This kind of systematic thinking springs from logical intelligence. Once a game gets rolling, kids need physical ability, strategic thinking, and negotiating skills. Winning and losing draw on interpersonal skills as the players take turns and take defeat. But most important, kids who learn to invent games never suffer the curse of boredom.

OBSTACLE COURSES

Building an obstacle course puts neglected bicycles, tricycles, and skates back in demand. Start with a safe, open space. Let kids design a track that dodges a series of objects. They can use cardboard boxes, crates, garbage cans, chairs, tables to go under, a wading pool, lumber for ramps, and potted plants, plus natural features like sloping driveways and curving sidewalks.

Safety first! Insist on inspecting the course before the first test run. And helmets, please! Maybe an adult with a stopwatch can be the official timekeeper and lifeguard.

CROQUET

Croquet is an obstacle course for a ball. So is miniature golf. Both are great for amplifying spatial and kinesthetic intelligence because players must consider speed, force, angles, terrain, and obstacles just to get the ball to its goal. Homemade croquet is easy. Just cut lengths of wire from coat hangers, bend them into arcs, and stick them in the ground. Make the mallets from a cube of Styrofoam stuck on the end of a yardstick, curtain rod, or broomstick. Or go to a thrift store and pick up an old golf club. Putters are just right for croquet or miniature golf.

GADGET GOLF

Designing a miniature golf course provides hours of inventive work before kids tee off. They can lay out a course in a living room or backyard, then create obstacles for the ball using household items. For example, cut both ends out of a coffee can and tip it over for a horizontal "hole." A book spread like a tepee or a piece of cardboard folded in half creates a little tent at which to aim. Other possibilities: Drive the ball between the legs of a chair, through a paper-tube tunnel, into a boot lying on its side. Ramps made of cardboard, a cookie sheet, or a cutting board increase the challenge. Miniature golf is a solo sport that's even more fun with two or three players. Agreeing on the rules is part of the learning experience.

TABLETOP MAZE

This game looks like a cross between pinball and a séance. Kids design a maze on a tabletop, then tip the table to propel a marble or ball toward the finish line. You probably won't want to tie up the kitchen table for days, so suggest that they use a card table, wooden board, or sturdy piece of cardboard. Now kids just need stiff paper cut into strips about one inch wide.

Stand the strips on edge and tape them securely to the tabletop to form curbs, walls, chutes, tunnels, and alleys—a path of obstacles through which the ball careens.

As kids lift or tilt the table to guide the ball through the labyrinth, they're manipulating the variables of time, speed, motion, inertia, friction, angles, and refraction. They'll strengthen both eye-hand coordination and fine motor skills. A stopwatch adds to the fun if they compete for the fastest time.

SLING BALL

This is like airborne bowling. It's easy to construct, great for rainy days, and you never get a gutter ball. First, use a pushpin to hang a string from the middle of the top of a doorway. The string should almost touch the floor. Attach a round object to the end—a tennis ball, potato, orange, apple, or ball of yarn. In the doorway, set up a formation of objects ready to meet their fate. Use wooden blocks, plastic drinking glasses, plastic liter bottles, or empty milk cartons. The players stand back, grab the end of the pendulum and let it fly. Rules and scoring systems evolve as needed.

HALL BOWLING

Kids can recycle the equipment from Sling Ball to turn a hallway into a bowling alley. Set up the pins at one end of the hall. Get as far away as possible and take aim. Tennis balls are great for this but don't forget about yarn or a ball of socks.

SOXBALL

This is an indoor version of basketball, just right for a bedroom. Bend wire from a coat hanger into a horseshoe shape. That's the basket. Now bend down a few inches of wire on each end of the basket, hook the ends over the top of a door, and close the door. Roll up a pair of socks and . . . Play ball! This relatively quiet pastime won't endanger furniture or windows.

HOPSCOTCH

Hopscotch can be the rage if it's liberated from that boring T-shape. Suggest spirals, triangles, circles, or diamonds. Kids just need fat sidewalk chalk and some encouragement. When they get tired of hopping, they can use the chalked figure for shuffleboard by sliding a Frisbee with a broom. Adding up the numbers in the boxes exercises their math muscles.

INSTANT ALTITUDE

Kids love the higher elevation and the weird Frankenstein walk that comes with mastering stilts. The easiest stilts to make are the coffee-can type held on with a bridle of rope or twine. Just get two one-pound coffee cans. Place them with the open end down. Poke a hole on each side of the can at the top. String twine or rope through the holes, then up into a loop that just reaches a child's hands. They step on the cans and yank on the leash. The rest is practice. Stilt-walking improves balance and coordination.

SOUND EFFECTS

This isn't so much a sport as a way to reinvigorate bike riders with a bit of noise. Get a clothespin and a playing card. Clip the card on the frame of the bike so it hits the spokes of the wheel as they go by. It produces a marvelous clacking sound that changes as kids speed up and slow down. For more noises, get a kazoo, a string of jingle bells to hang from the handlebars, or a whistle. Kinesthetic kids will be in heaven.

> *Scooping away the gravel, we would expose the permafrost and create surfaces for the marble and top seasons. These came in their turn each spring. It would be marbles for a while—and then, one day, tops. Followed a few weeks later by yo-yos. The yo-yo season was the apex of the social year.*
>
> *Chicago Days, Hoboken Nights*
>
> — DANIEL PINKWATER

MARATHONS, TRIATHLONS, AND OTHER SILLY STUFF

Try combining several sports. How about croquet on stilts? Or blowing a Ping-Pong ball through the tabletop maze—no hands, please!—or kicking a soccer ball along the obstacle course? Increase the challenge of regular games by switching muscle groups. The dominant muscles (right or left) get a rest, the other side of the brain gets a workout if kids reverse hands or feet while bowling or hopscotching.

SPORTS SECTION

Reading the sports section may snare a reluctant reader who only likes words if they're printed on the back of his shirt. Or try these books:

Angel and Me and the Bayside Bombers, by Mary Jane Auch. Brian is kicked off the soccer team and decides to form his own team.

Baseball Fever, by Johanna Hurwitz. Ten-year-old Ezra tries to convince his scholarly father that his baseball fever is not wasting his mind.

The Babe & I, by David Adler. A boy who is selling newspapers during the Depression to help his family meets Babe Ruth.

Sea Glass, by Laurence Yep. A Chinese-American boy whose father wants him to be good in sports finally asserts his right to be himself.

BOREDOM BRIGADE

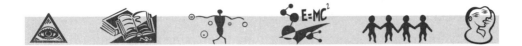

In our rush to sign kids up for tutorials and enrichment galore, we've nearly extinguished the spontaneous exercise of the imagination. It seems that there's simply no time to waste on fantasy when kids could be huffing and puffing through phonics worksheets or drilling on the times tables.

The surprise is that goofing around is good for the mind. Researchers believe that play, especially imaginative play, is an important component of intellectual and emotional development. It weaves together logic, aesthetics, narrative fiction, autobiography, emotions, and elements of the real world. When kids imagine, they integrate all their intelligences to create unique stories.

What's ironic is that imaginative play frequently springs from boredom. The brain craves stimulation—noise, food, movement, light, or thoughts. When there's a lull, the brain prospects for an idea, makes some connections, and finally seizes upon an activity. In the process, boredom disappears.

CRY BOREDOM

So boredom's a good thing. Unfortunately, hearing "I'm bored" scares some parents to death. They quickly fire off a volley of suggestions. The kid lobs them back like a big leaguer at batting practice: "I've already done that." "I hate Monopoly." "I'm out of paint." "All my friends are gone." "It's too hot." "It's too cold."

You can't fix boredom for your kids, and trying just gets in their way. Kids conquer boredom by tapping into *their* creative stores, *not yours.*

Think of it this way: You set out on a family hike, but the instant the hills get steep you hear whimpers of "Carry me." If you pick your child up, your muscles grow, his atrophy. The same applies to boredom.

Next time your kids whine that they're bored, relax. Say, "Good. That means your brain's looking for something interesting to do. I'm sure you'll find it soon."

YOUR ROLE IN THE IMAGINATION GAME

With that warning in mind, there are still some important ways to encourage imaginative growth while staying on the sidelines. Try these:

⇢ Limit TV viewing. That frees up time for creative play. Watching television substitutes an externally generated fantasy world for one that could be created by your child.

⇢ Resist the urge to provide entertainment for your kids. That's their job.

⇢ Let kids have solitude to develop imaginative thinking by daydreaming.

⇢ Help their attention span develop naturally by allowing plenty of time for kids to become actively engaged in a task without interruptions.

⇢ Show active interest in your child's thoughts and creative efforts. Treat their inventions with delight and respect.

⇢ Be patient with the process. Children are very vulnerable when they're creating their own worlds. They may abandon their creative efforts altogether if your response is persistently dismissive or critical.

IMAGINARY STRUCTURES

Draping sheets and blankets over tables and chairs is a venerable form of child architecture that calls upon kinesthetic and spatial intelligence. So if your kids decide they want to spend the morning in a mountain cave, open the linen closet, surrender your furniture, and they're in business. They can make tents, cabins, schools, and castles. Furnishing is easy: pots and pans, food, stools, pillows, and toys.

Sofa cushions create bulky, squishy structures such as forts, dungeons, or hideouts. Cover over the top with blankets or sheets; then kids can crawl inside with a flashlight for reading, coloring, or secret games.

IMAGINARY IDENTITIES

Most children try out a variety of roles during pretend games. In a single day they may be a teacher, bus driver, puppy, or Power Ranger. At the age of four my son regularly morphed into a jaguar with magic powers or the Helping Elf when it was time to clean his room.

This kind of imaginary play lets kids test-drive different personalities, using interpersonal and intrapersonal intelligence to construct scenarios and act out fantasy lives. They can be middle-aged at one moment and return to infancy the next. Provide simple props such

> *"Once I took all the wooden clothespins from my mother's laundry basket, spread them out over a large blanket, and dipped each one in the jar of mustard. . . . Proud of my hot-dog stand, I waited eagerly for my youngest brother, George, to get home from school so we could play hotdog vendor. I saw nothing wrong in what I did, and when my mom's screams were followed by blows from one of my dad's large leather belts, my bruised feelings hurt worse than the physical pain she inflicted.*
>
> *Growing Up in the Sanctuary of My Imagination*
>
> — NICHOLASA MOHR

79

> *The child pedaled furiously knowing perfect flight was simply a matter of time.*
> — UNKNOWN

as dress up clothes, hats of all kinds, shoes, purses, ties, and briefcases to assist their metamorphosis.

IMAGINARY OCCUPATIONS

Kids like to feel grown-up, so many of their pretend games imitate adult work. In the course of their games they may be exploring the beginning of a career or formulating goals for far-off adulthood.

DRIVERS

Lewis Carroll, creator of *Alice in Wonderland,* grafted a barrel to a wheelbarrow to create a miniature train system for his siblings. It ran along the garden paths, where stations were set up for passengers. He wrote a list of rules, including that the station master must mind his station and supply refreshments. He could put anyone who behaved badly in prison.

With a few rows of chairs, kids can play bus driver, train conductor, or subway motorman. A large cardboard box can be a boat, covered wagon, space capsule, or car. Wagons and tricycles can be combined to make a motor home for a pretend vacation or a float in the Rose Parade.

OFFICE WORKERS

Most kids have no experience with office work, but they love shuffling papers for an imaginary business. Get a cardboard box and throw in junk mail, used envelopes, receipts, bills, and phone books. Then go through your desk to see if you have a date stamp, stapler, rubber stamps, one-hole punch, envelopes of all sizes, rulers, pencils, and pens. If you have an old phone or calculator, the kids will be in business. Playing office taps linguistic and interpersonal intelligence with every imaginary transaction.

SNACK JOCKEYS

Here's another language-building activity that also lets kids practice social skills. To play restaurant, kids need waiter props, including an order pad, plates, a towel for a tablecloth, paper napkins, utensils, and a chalkboard or piece of cardboard to write their menu. For the kitchen staff, gather up canned goods, cereal boxes, egg cartons, spatulas, plastic utensils, and pots and pans. Kids can cut food pictures from old magazines and glue them on paper plates or use real food when it's time to serve. To make it more authentic, save bags, cups, or boxes from a fast food chain to recycle for imaginary mealtimes.

Alone by the river, alone through the fields, alone in the depths of the Five Hundred Acres, alone on the top of the forest. Sitting alone on the grass in the sunshine. Walking alone through the woods at night. Alone with myself. Alone—yet never lonely. What bliss this was.

The Enchanted Places
— CHRISTOPHER MILNE

SHOPKEEPERS

Kids just need to open the kitchen cupboards to play store. They usually spend lots of time organizing their shelves and making paper money before they're ready to open for business. An old utensil tray or jewelry box makes a good cash register. This activity is rich with math and language development.

> *I was a motor-car, to the dismay of my parents. Psychiatry was in its infancy then, both expensive and centered in Vienna. There was no one yet qualified to exorcise an internal combustion engine from a small boy . . .*
>
> *I switched on in the morning, and only stopped being a car at night when I reversed into bed, and cut the ignition.*
>
> ### Dear Me
>
> — PETER USTINOV

IMAGINARY FRIENDS

My brother Bob had an imaginary friend named Mergatroid for several years. We alternately laughed at and encouraged his Mergatroid tales.

Kids have imaginary friends for fun and companionship. When no one's around, they simply make someone up. Sometimes it soothes loneliness or makes them feel more competent. Some kids use their companion to communicate their needs or feelings indirectly to the adults in their lives. Mergatroid's job was to take the blame.

Although people used to worry about children with imaginary friends, researchers generally see this as a sign of mental health. Children with imaginary friends seem less shy and more able to focus their attention. Many have advanced social skills when compared with other children.

RETHINKING PLAYTIME

The following is a rigorous unschedule for creative growth that puts kids in the role of boredom-busters.

Monday	Pretending
Tuesday	Imagining
Wednesday	Daydreaming

Thursday	Browsing
Friday	Being bored
Saturday	Rescuing themselves
	from boredom
Sunday	Resting and ruminating

BOOKS ABOUT FANTASY AND PRETEND

Faith and the Rocket Cat, by Patrick Jennings. About a girl, her cat, a spaceship, and a dog who can write.

When the Sun Rose, by Barbara Berger. An imaginative girl's friend arrives in a yellow rose carriage and they spend the day painting and reading.

The Night It Rained Pancakes, by Mirra Ginsberg. Ivan tries to convince his brother of impossible things.

No Flying in the House, by Betty Brock. Mrs. Vancourt allows a tiny talking dog and a girl to move into her home.

The Minpins, by Roald Dahl. Billy wanders into the forest and discovers a civilization of tiny tree people.

The Night of the Golden Plain, by Mollie Hunter. A boy daydreams of becoming a fearless knight, doing good deeds and having great adventures.

The Wizard of Oz, by L. Frank Baum.

> *In all our efforts to provide "advantages" we have actually produced the busiest, most competitive, highly pressured and over-organized generation of youngsters in our history—and possibly the unhappiest.*
>
> *Eda LeShan*
>
> — THE CONSPIRACY AGAINST CHILDHOOD

83

FIVE

EXPLORING AND DISCOVERING

Getting Smarter with Odds and Ends

Visual / Spatial

Verbal / Linguistic

Musical

Kinesthetic

Logical/Mathematical

Interpersonal

Intrapersonal

85

JUNKYARD GENIUS

You've probably heard that necessity is the mother of invention. Well, junk is the father.

The history of invention is littered with people who really appreciated refuse. While in junior high, Orville Wright built a printing press with parts scrounged from a junkyard, including an old tombstone, firewood, and the hinged bars from a buggy.

Richard Feynman, Nobel physicist, sat before the TV cameras, dropped a ring of rubber into a glass of cold water, and pulled it out, misshapen. The cause of the *Challenger* explosion was revealed. His extraordinary insight into why machines work or fail began in a childhood of tinkering with junk. It grew into an obsession—"the puzzle drive." Feynman was bent on understanding the mechanical world by taking it apart.

Sadly, most of us buy, use, and discard machines without the faintest idea of how they work. Tons of unblemished plastic, miles of wires, millions of gears, and other fascinating fiddly-bits are all thrown away with the casual justification that "it costs more to fix it than to buy a new one." But there's an education in that junk.

JUNKYARD 101

Dismantling is a complex thinking process, but most seven- or eight-year-olds are up to the challenge. Taking things apart lets kids exercise their logical, kinesthetic, and visual intelligence. Direct sensory contact—touching, pushing, pulling—helps them discover the rules governing objects like gears, circuits, levers, pistons, springs, and switches. This purposeful handwork is the most powerful way to activate logical thinking and the surest way to retain it.

Kids who deconstruct make hunches, test ideas, and try again, which is exactly how scientists go about their work. They strengthen eye-hand coordination, patience, memory, and persistence, skills they need for practical real-world problem solving and for success in school. But it's their flexible thinking that allows them to transform and invent. So the next time you're about to donate a defunct Mixmaster or ancient Hoover to the Dumpster, STOP!

GETTING STARTED

It's easy to turn your broken radio, alarm clock, fan, blow-dryer, or scale into a project that could fascinate kids for days. Stow it in a low cardboard box. This becomes a natural work space and contains the mess. You can slide it under a bed or stick it on a shelf between work sessions without a lot of clean-up nagging. Kids can explore all they want and you'll be spared that machine-gun rattle of the vacuum cleaner choking its way across the floor. If the appliance won't fit in a box, lay down an old sheet, blanket, or tablecloth. Again, it will contain the chaos.

What else do you need? A set of screwdrivers. You can get these at a yard sale or thrift store for a song. Grandpas usually have some that they're happy to share. A dull table knife will also work, but you'll need at least

> *"I bought radios at rummage sales. They were old, broken radios and I'd buy them and try to fix them. Usually they were broken in simple-minded ways—an obvious wire hanging loose, or a coil was broken or partly unwound—so I could get some of them going.*
>
> *Surely You're Joking, Mr. Feynman*
>
> — RICHARD FEYNMAN

one Phillips screwdriver with the cross-slot bit. You might tuck some small jars or Baggies into the box for sorting and collecting parts.

SAFETY FIRST

A few safety precautions are in order. Remove the electrical cord and you won't have to worry about shocks. If you decide to leave the cord on, review the ground rules for anything that has to do with electricity. Other precautions: Get a cheap set of plastic glasses or goggles to protect each child's eyes because once in a while, parts will fly when they're released. Pint-size work gloves are a good idea, too. And throw in a few Band-Aids. There might be cuts or scratches as children and machine tangle, but nothing that should deter them from this fascinating pastime.

Never insist that they put things back together.

THE INVENTOR'S BOOKSHELF

When kids get stumped or want to know more, go to the library and check out *The Way Things Work,* by David Macaulay. Crammed with X-ray drawings of machines, great diagrams, and explanations, it's a playground for a budding physicist or engineer.

Here's some fiction about inventing:

The Gadget War, by Betsy Duffey, is the story of Kelly, a girl with a desk full of tools and head full of ideas for inventions, who wants to be a "Gadget Wiz."

Almost Famous, by David Getz, tells of a ten-year-old girl who wants to become a famous inventor so she can find a cure for her brother's heart condition.

Herbert Binns and the Flying Tricycle, by Caroline Castle.

The Trouble with Dad, by Babette Cole.

Don't miss these books about real-life inventors:

The Real McCoy: The Life of an African-American Inventor, by Wendy Towle.

The Picture History of Great Inventors, by Gillian Clements.

The Kids' Invention Book, by Arlene Erlbach.

The Hidden Contributors: Black Scientists and Inventors in America, by Aaron Klein.

For more ideas about making something out of nothing, see the section "Inventions" in chapter 4.

COLLECTIONS

Your first reaction to this topic might be, "Right, just what I need. More stuff!" If your household is like most, you're already plagued with too many unintentional collections—old but beloved running shoes, magazines that refuse to walk to the recycling bin, dirty socks, abandoned athletic equipment, stuffed animals, live animals, neighbor kids, and junk.

So why encourage kids to collect?

Collecting is thinking made visible. It's how kids begin to make sense of the world. When they encounter something intriguing—say, the dark boat-shaped seedpod of a jacaranda tree or a luna moth—their brains immediately try to fit it into a category of familiar objects. Making that connection expands their definition of the familiar category—it has one more example in it. And the new object gains a context where it belongs. That's how knowledge is constructed.

THE SKILLS IT BUILDS

Sometimes collecting looks like random prospecting or prolonged browsing. It's so subtle that you might never guess how fast the wheels are turning inside a kid's head. In reality, collecting is an amalgam of four powerful intelligences closely bound together in the act of selective gathering.

Kids who collect tend to be visually and kinesthetically sharp. They rely on close observation along with a sensitivity to shape, color, and texture to identify potential collectibles. Then they sort, categorize, and organize for use or display. They use these same skills in school to perform science experiments and organize research papers.

Although collecting may look whimsical, there is a strong undercurrent of logical intelligence running through most collectors. They have a sensitivity to patterns in the world around them that's revealed in the way they arrange their collections. Collectors also tend to have a generous amount of intrapersonal intelligence. Independent and self-reliant, they like to spend time alone working on their collections. They know how to entertain themselves in creative ways.

TALKING TO YOUNG COLLECTORS

Kids collect things that appeal to them—shells, seedpods, leaves, rocks, insects, books, cards, old photos—things that are profoundly uninteresting to most adults. It's probably been ages since you've felt the urge to crouch down and capture a roly-poly bug. On the other hand, kids don't get why you need one more golf club or antique sugar bowl.

Watching kids collect and organize their treasures can tell you a lot about how their minds work. That's why it's so important to restrain yourself when your child stoops to pick up yet another bottle cap. Even if you have to stuff your fist into your mouth up to the third knuckle, try not to snarl, "You already have five hundred of those! What do you need with one more? I'm warning you. If I find that on the floor, I'm throwing the whole damn collection out!"

Instead, ask some good questions: *What makes that piece special? Why does it fit in your collection? Is it the same as or different from all the others? How old do you think it is? What do you like about it?* Remember, collecting is how kids develop their individual taste, sense of aesthetics, and passion.

But let's face it. All that passion can get pretty messy. And smelly. Remember the last time your kids brought shells home from the beach and forgot them for a week? Even the most hygienic collections tend to spill all over and lose their meaning. They become Hoover-food or disappear into a black hole in the closet. But there are ways to make collecting work for you and your kids.

CONTAINERS

Half the work of a good collection is mental. It takes visual and logical intelligence to organize bits and pieces into a coherent collection. Some fortunate designers spend their lives making sense of museum collections for visitors. So give kids lots of ideas for collection containers. It will honor their acquisitiveness and bring order to the chaos. You both win.

Most houses are full of receptacles: egg cartons, shoe boxes, plastic take-out containers, cardboard six-packs, muffin tins, sectioned candy boxes, silverware dividers, cigar boxes, old briefcases, matchboxes, makeup case, tool box, tackle box, lunch box, envelopes, Baggies, strawberry boxes, fanny pack, purse, glass jars, coffee cans, cookie tins.

LABELS

Kids like making labels because it's a way of announcing ownership: "I found these, I organized them. They're mine. This is how I see the world." Labels also create a real-life reason for practicing linguistic skills including researching, writing, and spelling. Labels can include the name of the object, the date, and the place found. Advanced collectors might enjoy learning the Latin names for plants or shells. Here are some intriguing plant names:

Hakea laurina	Sea urchin (common name of an evergreen shrub)
Rubus ursinus loganobaccus	Loganberry
Ulmus hollandica	Dutch elm
Quercus velutina	Black oak
Trifolium	Clover

My brothers' favorite plant—aspidistra!

BOOKS FOR YOUNG COLLECTORS

Sylvester and the Magic Pebble, by William Steig.

Benny's Animals and How He Put Them in Order, by Millicent Selsam.

SOME OTHER BENEFITS

Collecting almost any natural object promotes an appreciation of natural beauty. The delicate structure of shells, the patterns in pinecones and bark, the sheer variety of leaves in any given patch of forest—all these inspire wonder and respect for our fragile environment.

Collecting transforms simple neighborhood walks into adventures. Set out around the block with the typical youngster and within five minutes you'll hear: "I'm tired." "When can we go home?" "Can you carry me?" But give a child an empty six-pack carton and a magnifying glass and he or she develops an intense fascination for the sidewalk and gutter.

> *An elderly uncle asked, "Well, what do you want to be when you grow up?"*
>
> *I loved to pick through trash piles and collect empty bottles, tin cans with pretty labels, and discarded magazines. The most desirable job on earth sprang instantly to mind. "I want to be a garbage man," I said.*
>
> *Growing Up*
>
> — RUSSELL BAKER

WHERE IN THE WORLD?

I'm not sure why maps fascinate kids, but I know they do. Maybe it's the sight of their whole world shrunk down to the size of a bath mat. Maybe it's the way maps raise questions: *Where does Grandma live? How about Uncle Richard? Why are some words on the map so small? Why are some countries so big?*

FINGER-TRAVELING

The best way for kids to learn about maps is to wallow on them. Tables are good work spaces but sprawling on the floor also suits serious finger-travelers. Throw in a magnifying glass, rulers, and marking pens and they'll create their own fun.

After some random cruising, kids start to concoct fantasy trips: *How do we get to the Grand Canyon? Which roads should we take? Is there anything to see along the way? How far is an inch, anyway?* And of course, *How long till we get there?*

Poring over maps strengthens visual intelligence, particularly the ability to read symbols. It's a real opportunity for kids to practice visualizing as an aid to memory and learning. Lingering over the colors, shapes, and location, they can learn to identify states, countries, and continents, so they'll really shine in geography lessons.

MAPS APLENTY

Scavenging for maps is easy because we're a map-loving country. Let's start with the freebies: maps at theme parks, car rental counters, train stations, and bus stops, in airline magazines and the telephone book. Drop by the local historical society, chamber of commerce, or tourist information center for more. Back issues of *National Geographic Magazine* are loaded with maps. You can get them for a song at used book stores, which may also carry prints or calendars of maps. For a small fee, try the Automobile Association of America and gas stations. Don't forget maps of the ocean floor, the surface of the moon, and the galaxies beyond.

MAPPING THE PAST

Maps from the thirteenth through the fifteenth century show more than just land and sea. They're illustrated with the hopes and fears of the mapmakers—demons, sea monsters, dog-faced men, and gold nuggets the size of grapefruit. If you look at lots of old maps, you can watch the edges of North America come into focus as explorers pushed their voyages of discovery. Studying old maps develops logical intelligence as kids notice patterns of where cities did and didn't spring up and the relationship of resources to population growth or colonization.

UNCERTAIN, TEXAS, AND OTHER PLACE NAMES

Avid map-readers discover city names that seem to be lifted from a novel or comic book. Aromatic Creek, Frostburg, Purgatory Peak, Yum Yum, Ding Dong, and Welcome. I swear—they're for real. The index of an atlas is a great place for kids to find unusual place names. Visit a used book store to buy old atlases cheap. Map reading builds linguistic intelligence. Initially, map readers practice the simplest form of reading: decoding single words. They add to their vocabulary and build their store of geographic knowledge. Finally, kids begin to ask questions about the meaning and origin of city names. See if you can find *American Place Names: A Concise and Selective Dictionary for the Continental United States of America,* by George R. Stewart, which tells the stories behind the words on a map. The name of Tesnus, in Tennessee, is "sunset" spelled backwards.

GET THE PICTURE

The quickest way to bring a map to life short of hopping in the car is to round up a pile of *National Geographic*s. They're a garage sale staple.

Or try a used book store, where they tend to pile up in dusty corners. Kids feast their eyes on the spectacular photographs and then locate the places on their maps. They can catch a bad case of wanderlust and a good sense of other cultures just flipping through the pages. The natural features of the earth, a sense of the beauty and variety of its people, a deep awe and curiosity about the world get etched into their minds as they browse and read.

FOLLOW ME

When I was little, we'd make treasure maps of the backyard and bury something "valuable." We could kill an afternoon planning, drawing, and searching. Once your kids grasp the essentials of cartography, suggest that they make maps of their own: treasure maps for friends to follow, neighborhood maps from home to school, maps of imaginary worlds. This creative activity develops spatial and logical intelligence by challenging kids to apply what they've learned about scale, estimating, graphing, measuring, and direction to a practical task. The test of their success is when other kids can navigate successfully following their maps.

WHERE IS NORTH, ANYWAY?

If you have kids who love gadgets, put a compass in those curious hands and let 'em go. This is primarily a do-it-yourself sport where kids spend hours discovering that they're heading south. Using a compass is a spatial exercise that weaves math and movement into a practical task. A trip around the block is a real adventure. To locate a relatively inexpensive compass, try a toy store, camping or sports outfitter, or a map, travel, or gizmo store.

ORIENTEERING

If your child is fascinated with maps and compasses, see if there's an orienteering club in town. Orienteers use maps to find a series of control points where their entry card is punched or checked. Whoever finds all the points first, wins. Orienteering is popular in rural or wooded areas but can be done on city streets, in neighborhoods, or in a park.

ARMCHAIR TRAVELING

Here are a few books set in famous locations. You and your kids can take an extended after-dinner junket without ever leaving home.

> *Brighty of the Grand Canyon,* by Marguerite Henry. A pack mule works the trails in the Grand Canyon.

> *Misty of Chincoteague,* by Marguerite Henry. A horse story set on an island off the coast of Virginia.

> *Paddle-to-the-Sea,* by Holling Clancy Holling. A toy boat sails across the Great Lakes and out the St. Lawrence Seaway.

> *The People in Pineapple Place,* by Anne Lindbergh. A boy moves to Washington, D.C., and is helped by seven invisible children.

> *Curious George and the Hot Air Balloon,* by Margaret and H. A. Rey. Curious George visits Mount Rushmore.

> *I began to read—no, I began to consume—*National Geographics, *with their pictures of glowing Lapps and mist-shrouded castles and ancient cities of infinite charm. I wanted to be a European boy. . . . I wanted to step outside my front door and be somewhere.*
>
> *The Lost Continent*
> — BILL BRYSON

Child of the Owl and *The Imp That Ate My Homework*, by Laurence Yep. Both stories are set in San Francisco's Chinatown.

The Fantastic Flying Journey, by Gerald Durrell. Great-uncle Lancelot takes his niece and twin nephews on an extraordinary journey around the world.

The Seven Treasure Hunts, by Betsy Byars. Two boys make up treasure hunts for each other with disastrous and hilarious results.

YELLOW PAGES

Have you ever lugged out the yellow pages to look for a taxi and heard yourself saying, "Taxidermist? Huh! I wonder what else is in here?" Ten minutes later you still don't have a ride to the airport, but you've discovered two must-see merchants in town.

THE CURIOSITY SHOPPER

The yellow pages are like a catalog for the curious. Little kids can let their fingers do the walking through the pictures. Older kids can browse the ads. Everyone can find something that begs to be investigated. A quick scan of my local directory suggested dozens of field trips where inquisitive kids can stretch their linguistic, interpersonal, and logical intelligence. Sign me up for the holography service!

aerial advertising	holography service
archery equipment	juke boxes
baker's equipment	music boxes
chimney cleaners	orchids
costume rentals	parachute jumping
dog training	piñatas
doll hospital	skywriting
dome structures	watchmaker's school
gemologist	weather vanes
gliding clubs	wood carving
grass skiing	worms

With a little research the yellow pages can lead you to enthusiasts and experts who'd be thrilled to share their knowledge, especially on a slow day. So give them a call to check location, hours, and whether kids are welcome.

These field trips are the time when kids with strong interpersonal intelligence really shine. They dust off their linguistic skills, especially in asking questions, and turn on the charm. For shyer kids, it's an opportunity to practice some important social skills like listening, asking questions, and making eye contact without much pressure. Their curiosity helps overcome their anxiety so they learn to get comfortable in new situations.

They learn to appreciate a variety of people. If you find a gregarious craftsperson, it's a great opportunity for kids to get a peek at a career. Kids discover that they can learn from lots of different people, not just teachers.

These interpersonal skills pay big dividends in classrooms where students are expected to collaborate on projects. Interpersonal intelligence is also critical in adult life, where the ability to see the world from another person's perspective is one of the most important predictors of success, while the lack of social skills and relationships constitutes a major health risk.

Before setting out, be clear with your kids that the goal of your visit is curiosity, not consumerism. This is a Look, Listen, and Learn event. Stay for fifteen minutes or an hour, depending on your child's age and level of interest. If you're really lucky, you'll have one of those I-never-knew-that moments. That alone makes the trek worthwhile.

OLD DIRECTORIES

If your child's fascinated with directories like the yellow pages, head for the reference desk of your main library and ask about business directories from the past. These local treasures list the name and job of everyone in town, so you may find an ancestor or two for your family tree.

The real charm of old directories is in the print ads, which give a glimpse of another era. Now, if only we had a time machine.

KITCHEN SINK CHEMISTRY

At the age of nine, Thomas Edison invested his entire allowance in chemicals, more than two hundred bottles' worth. Explosions stained his bedroom walls and ate holes in the carpet until his mom banished him to the cellar.

I got off easy. My son was content to mix "potions" in restaurants—ice water, a dash of salt, some cream, and as many sugar packets as we'd allow. He hoped the effect was magical but really it was chemical.

MIXED MESSAGES

Chemistry is the fast track to scientific thinking. Kids start with the question *I wonder what will happen if . . . ?* then proceed to experiment, observe, and draw conclusions. That's exactly what real chemists do. Fiddling with hyperactive liquids and powders stimulates logical, visual, and kinesthetic intelligence. Kids visualize the possibilities of baking soda and vinegar, then test them. If the experiment fails, the logical mind may step in to alter one or more elements and try again and again, using a methodical approach to discover the solution.

All the while, information is arriving through the senses. Weight, smell, color, and texture are clues about the relationship and behavior of materials. This sensory circus inevitably leads to cause-and-effect thinking, especially after a particularly dramatic explosion. Chemistry also taps into intuitive thinking as kids play out their hunches. When they repeat experiments, they notice patterns that represent the basic laws of nature. Finally, chemistry boosts concentration because kids can't wait to see what will happen next.

THE RIGHT START

With a budding chemist in the house, you're in for turbulent times. So brace yourself and lay down the laws about supervision, safety, and cleanup. Be clear about where, when, and with whom your wizard gets to work.

All the experiments that follow use simple household substances, but caution is required, especially where eyes are concerned. Sunglasses or plastic goggles will protect kids from splashes and accidentally rubbing their eyes with messy fingers. Add some plastic gloves and a man's shirt for a lab coat. Designate an area for experiments and let the good times roll.

BLOWING YOUR TOP

In a kid's head, Chemistry = Explosions. Here's a recipe for explosive rocketry that's safe and satisfying. You'll need a large plastic soda bottle and a cork that fits tight. Pour in a half cup of water and a half cup of vinegar. Put a teaspoon of baking soda on a small piece of paper towel and twist the packet closed like a wrapped hard candy. When ready to launch, drop the packet into the bottle, shove in the cork, step back, and get ready to cheer. For fun, attach a parachute to the cork or mount a little plastic person for a ride into space. Paint the cork a bright color or attach ribbons that will flutter as it falls. Kids can jiggle the formula to increase the force of the explosion and the height of the cork's flight.

THE SORCERER'S APPRENTICE

Kitchen chemists love fizz, so try this recipe for a cascade of bubbles. Put two cups of water in a plastic bottle with a tablespoon of baking soda and a little squirt of dishwashing liquid. Pour in a few teaspoons of vinegar and enjoy the foam.

MORE BUBBLE FUN

Bubble making seems like a fanciful game, but kids get fascinated with that circle of rainbow colors and soon they're toying with ideas about force and surface tension—simple fanciful physics. They can make their own bubble juice for a wand with this simple formula.

> 1 cup of water
> 1 tablespoon of dishwashing liquid
> 1 tablespoon of glycerin

If you can't find glycerin at the supermarket or pharmacy, substitute the same amount of sugar, corn syrup, or unflavored gelatin.

Double the recipe if you want to use a big wand to produce giant bubbles. Drag a slotted spoon, egg whisk, grater, or circle of wire through the juice and watch the bubbles fly. For more bubble recipes and experiments, check out *The Unbelievable Bubble Book,* by John Cassidy and David Stein.

BRIGHT AS A PENNY

Put a shine on old pennies by giving them a bath in salt and vinegar. After soaking for three to four minutes, they'll look like new.

> 1 cup vinegar
> ½ teaspoon of salt

Young Thomas Edison became interested in flight. He mixed a chemical mess which, if swallowed, he was convinced, would make anybody lighter than air. He tried to persuade his father's hired hand, Michael Oates, to take a dose and fly.

The Story of Thomas Alva Edison

— MARGARET COUSINS

OOBLICK

Kinesthetic learners adore ooblick, a fascinating mixture that's solid when you lean on it and liquid when the pressure's off. It can go from liquid to solid over and over, and that's what makes it fun. Mix a box of cornstarch with about two cups of water until it's as thick as mayonnaise. Put the mixture on a tray or in a low pan lined with foil or wax paper. As kids squeeze, pour, pinch and pound, they spout dozens of observations, hypotheses, and plain old shrieks of delight. Ooblick's amazing. **It also chokes plumbing,** so when your kids are finished, fold it all up in the paper liner and throw it in the trash.

CRYSTAL CROPS

Crystal gardens start to grow in a matter of hours, so here's a science project with instant gratification written all over it. You'll need to supervise a few minutes of "cooking" but most of the learning comes from watching crystals sprout in clear liquid. Have a magnifying glass or dime-store reading glasses handy to encourage close observation.

Start with giant alum crystals. Alum was once used to put the pucker into pickles. Look for it in the supermarket spice section. Add water and your kids can grow huge, chunky crystals in record time, so it's great for a rainy day when they're cooped up and looking for diversion.

Mix three-fourths cup of alum into two cups of water. Bring to a boil and stir until the alum is dissolved. Pour the solution into a heat-proof glass jar and let it cool for about an hour.

Now kids need to create a frame in which the crystal will grow. They can use a pipe cleaner or a plastic twist to form a star, triangle, a favorite letter or animal. Hang the shape from a string so it's completely submerged in the liquid but not touching the sides or bottom of the jar.

Watch the crystal grow. Within a few hours, kids will have a real rock. Let them experiment with hanging small objects like plastic animals or beads that they want to encase in crystal. Add more alum to the solution to repeat the process or speed it up.

Caution: This recipe produces a really strong solution, so be sure to tell kids this isn't the time to lick their fingers.

SIX

WORDSMITHS

Getting Smarter about

Thinking and Writing

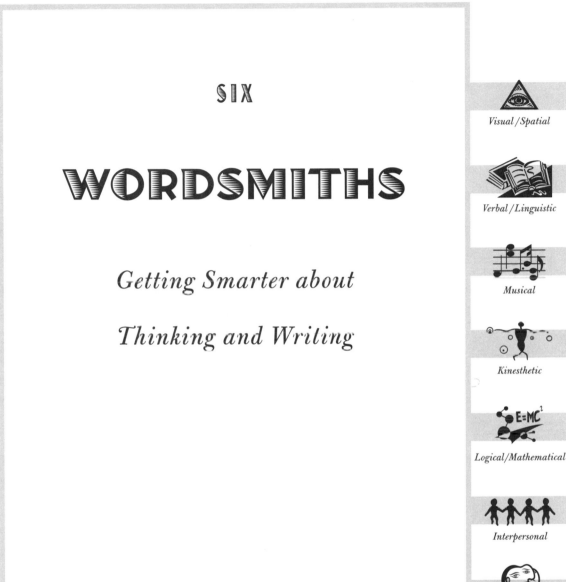

Visual /Spatial

Verbal /Linguistic

Musical

Kinesthetic

Logical/Mathematical

Interpersonal

Intrapersonal

THE POSTMAN'S PAL

Many people, kids and adults, hate to write—mainly because it's never brought them any satisfaction. They pick up a pencil, stare at the blank sheet of paper, and one thought comes to mind: "What's in it for me?"

That might have been the problem for Patsy Jefferson, a reluctant writer who received regular scoldings by mail from her father, Thomas Jefferson.

January 15, 1784

My Dear Patsy,

Your letter by the post is not yet come to hand. Your long silence had induced me almost to suspect you had forgotten me and the more so as I had desired you to write to me every week. I am anxious to know what books you read, what tunes you can play, and receive specimens of your drawings.

Unless you're a kid who's in love with words, writing is tough. It's slower and far more hazardous than talking. When you speak, nobody notices where you put your commas. Write, and they're after you with a red pencil.

PENMANSHIP

Since language is the basic tool of thought, any activity that features kids as producers and consumers of words is likely to help them speak and think in richer and more precise ways. The trick is getting them to pick up the pen and stay with it. One simple way is to put something in it for them. If they write and get something tangible back, the game is much more fun.

You can turn "I-hate-to" writers into the postman's pals if you introduce them to the world of freebies. There are thousands of companies, government agencies, and private enterprises that promote themselves by distributing free-for-the-asking items. Treasures in your mail slot for the price of a self-addressed stamped envelope and a simple letter of request.

This mail-order writing helps kids really understand the power of the written word. They scratch a few lines on a page, launch it into the postal system, and a distant receiver understands and responds. Mail-ordering also extends their awareness beyond their personal geography to learn about the world beyond.

MAIL-ORDER MANIA

Kids like mail-ordering because it makes them feel grown-up. Think about it. Most of the things kids own come directly from their parents. Getting those items usually involves a fair amount of negotiating, begging, and generally feeling little. With mail orders, they browse and choose without adult interference. When the mail comes with their own personal delivery, they charge back to the catalogs for more free stuff.

Publishing lists of free stuff has fueled a cottage industry in paperbacks that focus on kids as consumers. These books have simple formats, clear directions, enticing illustrations, and a huge array of free things. Some even include Internet freebies.

Check these out:

Freebies for Kids, by Jeffrey Feinman.

The Kid's Address Book, by Michael Levine.

Free Stuff for Kids, published by Meadowbrook Press, distributed by Simon & Schuster.

You don't even have to buy these books. Most libraries carry them in the kids' nonfiction section. What else will you need? Paper, envelopes, and stamps. That's it.

Here's a taste of what kids can get: posters, decals, pencils, trading cards, and postcards from major sports teams. Dozens of stickers, plus tattoos, jewelry, stamps, magazines, garden seeds, safety scissors, and magnifying glasses. Erasers, games, brochures, club memberships, pen pal lists, and how-to books. Notice that this activity isn't just about writing. In fact, what's entailed is a whole lot of reading, reading, reading. So you kill two birds with one stamp.

BEAUTIFUL LETTERS

If your young writer has an interest in fancy letters, calligraphy, the aesthetics of writing, encourage him or her to send for a free booklet called "Lettering" that shows alphabets in Gothic, Roman, old English and script. Send a large, self-addressed envelope to:

Carter Ink Company
Cambridge, MA 02167

STIFF CUFFS

My dear friend Christina Cocek adores words. She polishes her writing until it shines in the dark. Christina taught me how to play Stiff Cuffs, which became an instant favorite in my family, especially on long commutes. You start with a word pair—*stiff cuffs*—then the next person thinks of a word pair that starts with *cuff. Cuff links. Linksman. Manmade. Maidstone. Stone wall.* Think of verbal dominoes and you've got the idea. Any number can play until you hit a dead end. Then you start over.

WORD POWER

Word games are a powerful way to activate linguistic and logical intelligence. They build vocabulary, critical thinking, memory, and word retrieval skills. As a bonus, they're free, portable, and you can't lose the pieces. What more could a parent want?

I SPY

This simple observation game stimulates visual and logical intelligence. Kids just need eyes to play. "It" chooses something in plain sight and says, "I spy something blue." The players try to guess what it is by asking questions that can be answered by yes or no. *Is it bigger than my hand? Is it on a shelf? Is it something to eat?* The first one to guess the object is the new "It." This is great to play while stuck in the doctor's waiting room or when you get a slow-motion waitress. It promotes observation, listening, remembering, inferring, and reasoning. Plus, no messy cleanup!

TWENTY QUESTIONS

You can almost hear the gears turning when kids play this guessing game. It's harder than I Spy because the players only get twenty questions to identify the object, which doesn't need to be in plain sight. In fact, it doesn't need to exist. "It" can choose something invisible or even fictional, such as gravity, Santa Claus, or Darth Vader. Kids learn to start with general questions about size, use, fiction or nonfiction, location, living or non, then zero in on a smaller target by process of elimination. Players build linguistic skills, particularly their ability to use words precisely while applying rules of logic to the clues.

FAST TALK

This is a brain-and-tongue race where you select a category and kids rattle off things in that category until time's up. *How many zoo animals can you name in thirty seconds?* It's that simple. But it really sharpens language and logic tools, especially word association, classification, and retrieval. Some kids also hone their debate techniques trying to justify their choices. Then the conversation really heats up! Here are some starter categories: desserts, pets, jobs, tools, plants, foods, countries, winter clothes, sports, book titles, fairy tales, heroes, names of dogs that start with *S*. Once kids get the hang of the game, they'll discover a dozen more categories on their own.

PIG LATIN

Forget pigs! This game is strictly for mental gymnasts. Pig latin requires deconstructing and reconstructing words as they're pouring out of your mouth. Picture rotating the tires on a car as it's cruising down the road and you begin to grasp the challenge of speaking PL. Some kids love it so much they won't utshay-upway.

In a nutshell, pig latin has two rules. First, if a word starts with a consonant, take the first letter, shift it to the end of the word, followed by -*ay*. Second, if a word begins with a vowel, just add -*way* to the end of the word. Thus, "She loves to eat cookies" becomes "E-shay oves-lay oo-tay eat-way ookies-cay." It just takes practice.

Caution: If you ask your kid why his chores aren't done and you get a lively but unintelligible excuse in pig latin, don't blame me. At least his brain is working.

> *While waiting for a train, I amuse myself by scribbling down a list of the collective words in which our language is so rich, a pack of hounds, a shoal of fish, a peal of bells. There are about a hundred of them but I can seldom think of more than fifty.*
>
> *The Happy Traveller*
>
> — FRANK TATCHELL

RIDDLES

A riddle is a whodunit. It starts with a mass of facts and the trick is to whittle the possibilities down to a single answer. Riddles involve homonyms and plays on words, also logic and imagination. You probably had your favorites as a kid, like:

> *What has three feet but cannot walk?* A yard.
> *What's smaller than an ant's mouth?* What goes into it.
> *What has teeth but never eats?* A comb.
> *What has four eyes and runs two thousand miles?* The Mississippi.

Riddles can feel like a mental stress test. Tired adults rarely enjoy riddles, but kids snatch them up like candy. So if you start riddling with your kids, be sure to have a fistful on hand. Library shelves are crammed with riddle books. Expect no peace once your kids discover this.

PENCIL PALS

In the olden days, the mailman was the only commuter on the information superhighway. So everybody from Thomas Jefferson on down had pen pals. The telephone drove pen-palling to the brink of extinction, but it's making a comeback thanks to e-mail.

WHY WRITE?

Humans seem to have a deep need to connect with one another, whether friends, family, or colleagues. That's why they write letters. Corresponding springs as much from interpersonal and intrapersonal intelligence as from the linguistic regions of the brain. Kids as young as five or six can strengthen valuable writing skills by getting hooked on pen pals. The trick? Avoid the deadly "Dear Pen Pal" exercise by introducing unusual formats that don't feel like writing at all.

START SMALL

Post-its are perfect for first letters. Write small notes to your kids and stick them on their mirrors, doors, or lunch boxes. Not lists of chores but *Thank you* or *Wow! You're a great kid.* Give your child Post-its in assorted colors and see what kind of notes you get in return.

WISH YOU WERE HERE

Kids can share events in their lives easily and often, if you just expand their notion of stationery. Forget paper. It's much more exciting for kids to send off bits and pieces of their lives. Mail a page of the calendar with notes or sketches—*Grandma, Had a great week at camp. I learned how to swim.* Jot a few sentences on the program from a school play and drop it in the mail slot. Or tear pictures from the local paper and write a comment about the event. Five minutes and one stamp later, you've touched someone's life.

MEMORIES OF HOME

One of the most painful events in childhood is when best friends move away. Many kids never make the shift from playmate to pen pal because it's too hard to reduce a bike-riding, ball-playing, flesh-and-blood friendship to words on paper. If your child has lost a pal, suggest that they keep in touch by sending tourist postcards. The writing space is small enough that even reluctant writers can fill it in a few minutes The bonus is that the mover receives a reminder of home and the one left behind gets a glimpse of the friend's new town. With a roll of stamps and a pile of dime-store postcards you can nourish a long-distance friendship for years.

STORIES ABOUT LETTERS AND FRIENDS

> *Letters to Lesley,* by Janice Marriott. Twelve-year-old Henry plots to marry his eccentric mother to the wealthy father of his new pen pal.

> *Annie Bananie,* by Leah Komaiko. Annie is moving away and her best friend wonders if their friendship will survive.

> *When I was about eight years old, being fond of animals, I was not surprisingly a Dr. Dolittle fan; and one day I wrote to Hugh Lofting to say so. Partly I wrote because Nanny encouraged me to, partly I wrote because I really did want to say how much I liked his books, and I suppose that partly I wrote because I hoped I might get a letter back.*
>
> *The Enchanted Places*
>
> — CHRISTOPHER MILNE

Anna's Secret Friend, by Yoriko Tsutsui. Anna has just moved to the neighborhood and she misses her friends. Soon flowers, a note, and a paper doll arrive in her mailbox. At last she catches her secret friend.

Best Friends, by Steven Kellogg. Kathy feels betrayed when her best friend goes away to camp and has a good time without her.

A Letter to Amy, by Ezra Jack Keats. Peter wants his new friend Amy to come to his birthday party. He tries to send her a letter, but problems arise.

MAIL ART

Art is a powerful language, so encourage the artists in your family to make their own postcards. Start with a stiff piece of paper. Reserve one area for the stamp and address, another for a short message. On the flip side, kids can glue a favorite photograph or picture from a magazine. They can draw, paint, or sketch a cartoon.

Photos from summer vacations or the holidays make great postcards, too. Just glue them on a stiff piece of paper, print a message, and drop them in the slot. No envelope necessary. Did you know you can even send a coconut or basketball through the mail without a wrapper? If it has an address and the proper postage, it will arrive. Try it for fun.

STAR APPEAL

How many times have you heard adults gush about spotting a movie star, tennis pro, or senator? Glimpsing the famous is exciting, but getting a letter or photograph from a celebrity is the jackpot. Young autograph hounds just need *The Kid's Address Book,* by Michael Levine; it's a paperback locator device crammed with the names and addresses of celebrities, athletes, entertainers, politicians, organizations, and clubs.

FAMOUS PEN PALS

Reading other people's mail is frowned upon and usually boring, unless it's the published correspondence of famous people. Here are two unusual books of letters to and from children.

> *Dear Mrs. Parks: A Dialogue with Today's Youth.* Correspondence between Rosa Parks and American children who wrote asking questions and seeking guidance from the mother of the civil rights movement.

> *Letters to Children,* by C. S. Lewis. A collection of letters from the author of "The Chronicles of Narnia" to various children.

AUTHOR! AUTHOR!

When I was four, I opened a library for my dolls. The volumes were the size of postage stamps, with tiny pictures and scribbly text. I published a scrap-paper series about the things I drew best—horses, trees, and flowers. I still have a cardboard-bound first edition from my sixth year.

THE HUMAN PEN

Your kids can become authors long before they've labored through the alphabet if you're willing to be a human pen. Just form a write-and-draw team. They talk, you write, then they supply the pictures.

You may be wondering what kids learn if you do all the work. A surprising amount. For a start, dictating draws on the basic material of linguistic intelligence. Little dictaters learn to describe events accurately and include details. They practice a variety of sentence structures, develop story lines, and expand their vocabulary. Most important, they discover that writing is a tool for capturing ideas on paper, they can read and enjoy ideas over and over again.

A word of caution. You might be tempted to suggest adjectives or reorder kids' sentences along the way. It's really important that you resist the urge to edit. Novice writers remember exactly what they said and they get confused if you change the text.

MORE WAYS TO GROW WRITERS

At first, kids' books may sound a lot like their favorite bedtime stories. It's okay. Don't say, "Don't copy." Imitating is how we learn to walk, talk, play basketball, and write. Kids master storytelling in stages and eventually their own ideas emerge. So just keep reading aloud. Good books provide powerful how-to-write models that kids internalize. And don't forget, the most potent learning fertilizer is praise. When kids trot out a clever phrase or idea—pour it on.

FIRST EDITIONS, INC.

Once kids get hooked on seeing their ideas in print, you can graduate from pencil pusher to proud parent. Older kids like to explore who they are and how they feel, but in a very private arena. They are often drawn to journals and diaries because they're using writing as a tool for self-discovery. Be sure to see the sections "Keeping Secrets," in chapter 1; "Ancestor Maps," in chapter 2; and "The Play's the Thing," later in this chapter, for more ideas to promote intrapersonal intelligence through writing.

What do young writers need? A cozy place to write, great reviews when they publish, and basic supplies—paper, pencil, and staples. Add a ruler if they want lines for the text. And that's it. Try to use recycled paper. Gather up old business stationery, hotel notepads, flyers, envelopes, and junk mail. Greeting cards and wedding invitations are often printed on wonderful paper, much of which is blank. Save the usable parts and kids can design books with different paper for each page.

Short books first. That way kids don't run out of story before they run out of pages. For starters, cut a sheet of paper into four pieces and staple them together. Or tear a half dozen pages from a telephone message pad. Tiny spiral notebooks are also naturals for minibooks. Remind kids that they can write a few pages and add more as their ideas expand.

THE COVER-UP

A book cover is a declaration. It makes private writing public domain. Keep thinking recycling. Kids can make great book covers from card stock, recycled flyers, brown bags, wrapping paper, shirt cardboard, shopping bags, cloth, or photographs. Attach the cover with staples or clamps. Punch holes through the pages and thread them together with ribbon, yarn, pipe cleaners, or rubber bands. Kids love to cut out magazine letters for their titles.

BEGINNER'S BOOK LIST

A simple way to jump-start the writing process for kids is to suggest books of lists: *My Favorite Foods, Things I Like, My Friends.* The sentences follow a short, simple pattern, so first-time writers feel successful. Most of their effort goes into the illustrations. Sometimes these lists spontaneously shift into narrative when an idea is triggered. This is a really natural way for kids to grow as writers.

The first rule among writers is to write about what you know. So here are some starting points for young authors: books about their pets, vacations, trips to amusement parks, a new baby, a new house, school friends, visiting relatives, or winning at soccer.

Some kids won't pick up a pencil except to exercise their imagination. They like to write the type of nonsensical books that made Dr. Seuss famous. Suggest titles such as: *If I Had a Flying Horse, If I Were an Astronaut, Living on Mars, I'm in Charge of the World, If Pigs Could Fly.* If your child has an imaginary friend, suggest a biography. Ask questions like: What *does he look like? What's his favorite food? Where does he go while you're at school?*

IS THERE A HEMINGWAY IN THE HOUSE?

Although writing is a very solitary pursuit, fiction writers draw on their interpersonal intelligence to get inside their characters. Their ability to see things from another person's point of view lets them create convincing characters and write dialogue that expresses ideas and emotions.

When kids get into the fiction game, they're intuitively playing by the same rules as Mark Twain, Margaret Mitchell, and Ernest Hemingway. Fiction relies on five elements: character, plot, setting, conflict, and resolution.

You can help your child discover these elements by asking some simple questions.

- Character

Who's going to be in your story?
What does he/she look like?

- Setting

Where does your character live?
Where will the story happen?
Will your character go anyplace else?

- Plot

What's going to happen in the story?
What happens first? Next?
What else might happen to your character?

- Conflict

Does your character have any problems?
Does he/she have friends or enemies?
Does anyone get hurt, get lost, need help in the story?
Is anyone afraid, angry, worried? Why?

- Resolution

How does the story end?
How did the characters solve their problems?

Characters really come alive when kids learn to use dialogue in their stories. Just ask: *How do you think he/she would talk? Can you make his voice?* Maybe the character has an accent or whispers, or speaks pig latin. Dialogue makes reading aloud much more lively.

In her free time, she wrote stories. Before long she was designing book jackets to go with her stories. She even made books small enough to fit in her hand.

Rachel Carson:

Voice for the Earth

— GINGER WADSWORTH

Fiction writing is like quilting: it's great piecework. Kids can pick it up and put it down, let the characters act out for a while, then call intermission. Each writing session can be a new chapter.

HONORING BOOKS

Announce that kids' books are important by keeping them in a special place. You don't have to add on a room or even build a bookshelf. Just collect them in one place and visit there often. Keep a book box or basket next to the bed or chair where you read at night and read at least one child-authored book before switching off the light. Encourage older kids to read their books to younger siblings and younger writers to entertain Grandma on the phone.

A delightful introduction to the writer's life is *The Abracadabra Kid,* in which Sid Fleischman tells how he went from reluctant reader to Newbery Medal–winning author. It's a lively tale with lots of tips on how to get started in the writing game.

Another lovely book is *A Grain of Wheat,* by Clyde Bulla, in which Bulla describes his childhood on a Missouri farm and how he decided to become a writer.

IN THE MARKETPLACE

Kids who are serious writers may want to take the publishing plunge. Seeing their work in print can be a tremendous affirmation. Just be sure they're strong enough for rejection, too. If getting into print is their dream, try *The*

Market Guide for Young Writers: Where and How to Sell What You Write, by Kathy Henderson. It has over 150 listings for authors from eight to eighteen years.

TOP SECRET

Why is it that kids who hate reading devour comic books and beg for more? Or kids who despise writing become expert cryptographers and swap elaborate coded messages under your very nose? Some kids just need an intriguing format to put their literacy skills to work.

Of course, the real attraction is that codes equal power. Code writers share ideas without fear of exposure and feel superior to puzzled siblings and curious parents. Outsiders are out of luck.

LEARNING IN DISGUISE

So introduce your kids to spy language. While they're scratching out messages that look like a calculator with a stutter, they'll bolster their linguistic and visual intelligence. Junior cryptologists can't escape from grammar, spelling, and sentence structure. They're just disguised in an alternate symbol system. When kids start swapping secret messages with a friend, they have to translate symbols back to standard text. In effect, they're reading in *two* languages. Finally, code enthusiasts possess strong logical skills and the eyes of a hawk, since patterns are the key to any code.

CODES VS. CIPHERS

Technically, codes are whole words that replace other words. For example, Secret Service agents use code words like *the eagle* or *big bird* to refer to the president. What most of us call codes are really ciphers, where each letter is replaced by another letter or symbol. Both have been around since writing met espionage.

CAESAR CIPHERS

Around 3000 B.C. the Babylonians invented cuneiform writing. To send secret messages between cities, they wrote on the freshly shaved head of a slave, waited for the hair to grow out, and off he went. Upon arrival, he shaved again and had his head examined. Not exactly e-mail but it worked!

Julius Caesar used shift ciphers for dispatches. To build this code, write the alphabet on a line. Now choose a secret number. Suppose it's 5. Put your finger on *A* and shift over five letters. That would take you to *F*. Write the alphabet again, beginning under *F*. Here's how the code would look:

A B C D E F G H I J K L M N O P Q R S T U V W X Y Z

V W X Y Z A B C D E F G H I J K L M N O P Q R S T U

To encode words, replace each letter in the message with the letter below it. **DOG** becomes **YJB**. You can change the secret number anytime. A variation of this is the backward alphabet cipher. Write the alphabet forward, as above. Then underneath, write it backwards. When you encode, *A* is *Z*, *B* is *Y*, and *Z* is *A*.

NUMBER, PLEASE

Kids can use the same process as above but assign a number to each letter of the alphabet. The numbers can run in order from 1 to 26, so *A* is 1, *B* is 2, and so on. Or they can be scrambled like eggs. The coded message looks like a stock market printout.

HISTORIC CRYPTOGRAMS

Here's a code used by King Henry the Eighth in the sixteenth century, the Society of Freemasons in the nineteenth century, and the Confederate secret service during the Civil War. Chatting in this code stimulates visual intelligence and requires attention to detail that kids will rarely give to their spelling list.

To start, draw two tic-tac-toe grids. Leave one grid blank and put a dot in each of the nine compartments of the other grid. Now draw two Xs. Leave one as it is and again put dots in each of the four compartments of the other. This creates twenty-six distinct compartments, each of which can be assigned to a letter of the alphabet.

To write in this code, the letters of the alphabet are replaced by a drawing of the compartment they occupy in the diagram. The coded message looks like a series of right angles, arrows, or v's, some of which have dots in them.

DO-IT-YOURSELF SECRETS

Kids can make personal codes by writing the alphabet and assigning a symbol to each letter. For example, A = ★, B = 😖, C = ⌣, D = ↑, E = ≋, F = ◁, and so on. This is where the visually intelligent scribes really shine. Once a copy has been given to a friend, they're in the spy business.

I myself learned to read from comic books. I remember the actual moment when I became able to "code-bust," as they say. As a second-semester first-grader, I purchased a Batman comic—the first brand-new comic I ever owned. I had invested a dime. It was my own property. I was going to read every word in the thing or be damned.

Chicago Days,

Hoboken Nights

— DANIEL PINKWATER

DISAPPEARING INK

What could be more surprising than using a toaster to reveal an invisible message? The magic ingredients are right in your kitchen. Almost any citrus fruit juice (lemon, orange, or grapefruit) can be used as invisible ink. Onion juice also works well. Or try a half teaspoon of honey dissolved in a half glass of water.

Write with a tiny brush or a toothpick on absorbent paper. Heat the paper gently over a light bulb or toaster and a light brown message appears. A warm iron also works. Never use an actual flame. Kids need supervision for this step, but it's worth your time to see them conspiring to read and write.

BOOKS ABOUT CODES AND CIPHERS

READ-ALOUD CLASSICS

The Gold Bug, by Edgar Allan Poe, in which a man finds a message written in cipher on a piece of parchment buried in the sand along the shore. He decodes the message and it leads him to a treasure chest of pirate gold and jewels.

The Adventure of the Dancing Men, by Sir Arthur Conan Doyle, in which Sherlock Holmes decodes messages made up of tiny figures that look like dancing men.

The Chain of Death, by Maxwell Grant, creator of The Shadow of radio fame, includes many curious codes.

MORE BOOKS ABOUT CODES

Hieroglyphs for Fun: Your Own Secret Code Language, by Joseph and Lenore Scott.

Codes for Kids, by Burton Albert Jr.

THE PLAY'S THE THING

Kids usually get their first taste of playwriting when they grab a couple of stuffed animals and make them talk. Adventures follow. The cloth critters fight, make up, have babies, get lost and survive other indignities, all spun out of your child's imagination. This simple pastime relies on dialogue, the workhorse of playwriting. As kids reel off spontaneous scripts, they develop linguistic skills including vocabulary, emotional expression, and the ability to construct a story.

Dress-up is usually the next step in becoming a playwright. Costumes and props are among the strongest lures to imaginative play and language development. Decked out in oversize glory, kids take on all the roles: writer, director, costume designer, and actor.

If your kids don't have a dress-up kit, start one now. Just go through your closet and grab those space-wasters you'll never use again—the more outrageous the better. Hats certainly, scarves, T-shirts, belts, old jewelry, boots, vests, gloves, aprons. Put them all in a special container. An old picnic basket would be perfect. Or try a suitcase, footlocker, or laundry basket that's not getting much attention.

GETTING BEYOND PRETENDING

At first, kids think a play just means dressing up and pretending to be someone they're not. Other characters get involved, something happens, and then it's over. That's a good start, but you can extend their concept of play-acting by asking:

- Questions about the characters:
Who's in your story?
Is there a good or bad person in your play?
Is one character scary, mean, or smart?
How do the characters feel about each other?
Does your play have a hero?

- Questions about sequence:
Where are your characters at the start of the play?
What happens to them first?
What happens next?
Do they go somewhere else? Why?
What happens in the end?

- Questions about conflict:
Do the characters have a problem?
Who's causing the problem?
How do they try to solve it?
Who helps them?
Do they solve their problem?

SETTING THE STAGE

Producing a play allows visual learners to strut their stuff. The setting can be as simple as the front porch or the hearth. Encourage kids to take advantage of natural sets such as a patio, barn, or basement. Your garden may be the perfect scene for a jungle story. Indoor sets can be concocted by rearranging furniture or hanging a sheet for a backdrop.

Another approach is shadow plays—the literary equivalent of finger shadows on a wall. Visual and kinesthetic learners love the challenge of creating shadows that look like animals or people, then filling in the dialogue. For the full-body version, you'll need to help your shadow-actors string up a sheet or curtain. It needs to be pulled tight, so you might want to stretch it over a doorway and fasten it with thumbtacks. Take the shade off a lamp with a 100 or 150 watt bulb. Set it up behind the players and turn off all the other lights. They'll spend hours discovering which props, postures, or positions are the most effective in silhouette.

SCRIPTWRITING

Writing down the actual script may not happen until children are eight or nine. Or they may never commit their ideas to paper. This won't stop them from having some wonderful off-off-Broadway fun.

If kids want a written script, let them discover the format that works best. For example, when they realize that it's hard for more than two characters to read off one page, they'll improvise. Perhaps they'll tear the script into pieces. Players may copy out their own parts separately or just memorize most of their lines and rely on a prompter for cues. Thinking through these challenges strengthens visual, spatial, linguistic, and interpersonal skills.

STRIKE UP THE BAND

Creative kids will probably discover that some scenes would be better with sound effects—whistles, bells, jingling coins or keys, the doorbell, a door slamming, water faucets, an egg timer, or a drum, just to mention a few. And

> *The Alcott girls put on plays in the barn with an ever changing cast of dolls and cats. Like the colorful characters she would later create, Louisa's babies were "fed, educated, punished, rewarded, nursed and even hung and buried." One Concord playmate remembered that Louisa's theatrics made his "sides ache with laughter."*
>
> *Keeping Secrets*
> — MARY LYONS

don't forget music. What's a play without an overture? Kids can tape-record their audio effects in advance or just sound off as the action unfolds.

PLACES, PLEASE

A play's a lot of work, so let your kids know that you respect their creative efforts. Have a theater party. Rearrange the chairs and invite neighbors or relatives. Encourage kids to design programs or cut bits of paper into tickets. Simple refreshments such as popcorn, cookies, and juice make it a festive occasion. Then sit back, drink in the scenery, and clap like mad.

THE REAL THING

How can curious kids get a sniff of the greasepaint or a peek behind the footlights? Almost every junior high or high school has a drama club, with plays intended for families. Their productions are often excellent and always inexpensive. Check out the community playhouse or watch for open-air productions in the park, grab a blanket and go. If there's a big theater in your town, see if they have tours or an open house where kids can go backstage, see sets being built, and visit the costume room.

If you seem to have a budding actor on your hands, small theater companies occasionally cast children. This wonderful opportunity for a child requires real commitment from parents. You'll be sitting through every rehearsal and production, even if your trouper's only in the limelight for two minutes. Theater parents are a truly dedicated lot.

THEATER BOOKS

Every time you read good literature to your kids, you're exposing them to the basic elements of a play. But for a lot of laughs about some young actors, read *The Best Christmas Pageant Ever,* by Barbara Robinson. The mean Herdman kids get involved in the community Christmas play. Your kids will want to hear this one over and over again.

For a look at life in the theater long ago, read *An Actor's Life for Me,* by Lillian Gish. Miss Gish recounts her childhood in the theater around 1900, before movies were invented. Also look for books about William Shakespeare and the Globe Theatre.

SEVEN

FINGERSMITHS

Getting Smarter through

Handmade Tasks

Visual/Spatial

Verbal/Linguistic

Musical

Kinesthetic

Logical/Mathematical

Interpersonal

Intrapersonal

PUPPETS

Kids of a certain age love any excuse to misbehave. With a puppet in hand, they can be rude and noisy and smack everything in sight.

Happily, puppet shows are more than a chance to abandon good manners. These spontaneous dramas tap into a wide range of intelligences and develop skills that translate directly into success at school. It's easy to see the connection between puppets and linguistic intelligence. Puppeteers invent characters, plot, and dialogue. Their stories need a beginning, middle, and end, so they're manipulating the basic tools of the writer's trade.

Puppeteering also provides a perfect means of developing interpersonal and intrapersonal intelligence, because kids get to express emotions and try on different roles. A good child plays the meany. The littlest kid gets to be the hero. They can act out fantasies without the risk of criticism because they're shielded by their puppet.

READY-MADE PUPPETS

The simplest puppets are recycled dolls and stuffed animals on sticks. Use string to lash the doll or critter to one end of a yardstick. Puppeteers grab the other end of the stick, crouch down behind a table or couch, and perform on the furniture.

If kids want a marionette effect, tie strings to a doll's hands and feet, then attach the strings to overhead handles. Use chopsticks, wooden spoons, or even a thin branch. Manipulating marionettes challenges kinesthetic and spatial intelligence as kids experiment to discover how the jerk of a string translates into credible and expressive movements for their characters. A floor or tabletop makes a fine marionette stage.

GLOVE PUPPETS

Kids can make instant puppets from old gloves, oven mitts, or socks. First, they should stick their hands in and experiment with movements to get a sense of the character. Then they can use a marking pen to draw the features. Add buttons for the eyes and yarn or raffia for hair. Decorate rubber gloves with permanent marking pens for waterproof puppets that perform in the bathtub.

SPUD PUPPETS

Stick a potato on the end of a pencil, chopstick, or handle of a wooden spoon. The rest is pure imagination. Straight pins or toothpicks are all you need to attach hair and features. Think of using raisins, dried fruit, grapes, Cheerios or marshmallows, Easter basket grass, felt, buttons, pipe cleaners, and ribbons to complete the character.

PULP PUPPETS

Here's another fail-proof approach to puppet making using kitchen cupboard materials. Paper lunch sacks can be used in two ways. Stuff a bag with newspaper to make a puppet head. Then tie it shut at the bottom and insert a stick to control the puppet. A simple drape around the stick will hide the puppeteer's hand. Or stuff baby clothes to make a body.

Want a talking puppet? Flatten the bag, stick your hand inside, and tuck your fingers in the little flap at the bottom of the bag. The puppet "talks" when the fingers move. Glue eyes, nose, and upper lip to the bottom of the bag. Teeth, tongue, and lips can be added under the flap, and arms and legs glued to the body of the bag.

Kids can mass-produce very simple puppets by tracing around cookie cutters shaped like people or animals. Then the paper figures can be cut out and mounted on sticks, with as much coloring and decoration as needed to create the characters. Making and using paper puppets develops eye-hand coordination and language skills.

MEDIA PUPPETS

Older kids like realism. They may want a movie idol in their puppet show. No problem. With a pile of magazines they can recruit anyone from a president to a hockey player. To make realistic-looking puppets, they just cut out full figures or faces of famous people and glue them on sticks. Then they can write a script for their hand-picked cast, using current events or fantasy as their source material.

JUMBO PUPPETS

What about a body-size puppet? Kids love hugeness, so suggest a pillowcase stuffed with socks or towels for a head. Stick a broomstick up into the center of the head. Tie it tightly at the neck. Now tape a coat hanger to the stick at the neck. Hang clothes on it and you have an almost life-size puppet. Don't forget about jewelry, a hat or wig, glasses or a Halloween mask to bring the character to life.

SETTING THE STAGE

The simplest way to stage a puppet show is to hide behind a couch or a table covered with a sheet. Another solution is to put a tension-mounted curtain rod in a doorway and hang a tablecloth, sheet, or curtain over it for an instant screen. Adjust the height to your puppeteer. If puppets become the rage in your house, kids can devise a more permanent theater with a box from a large appliance. Cut a door in one side or just let them lift the box up and crawl inside. Cut a window in the front for the performance space. Hang curtains on a string inside the opening. Puppeteers can apply a coat of paint and design a marquee for each new show.

PLACES, PLEASE!

Add to the fun of the play by suggesting a sound track. It can be as simple as playing music at the beginning and end of the performance. Or add sound effects using pots and pans, drums, horns, whistles, or bells. Don't forget the most important sound—applause.

Charles loved drama and devised a puppet theater for his brothers and sisters. With the help of his family and the village carpenter, he made a troupe of marionettes and a stage. He wrote plays for the puppets and produced the shows, handling the complicated puppets himself.

Very Truly Yours,
Charles L. Dodgson,
Alias Lewis Carroll.

— LISA BASSETT

PULP FICTION

When mass-produced paper hit Europe it transformed the world of communication, giving us Leonardo da Vinci's sketchbooks and Shakespeare's folios. Even now, in the age of electronic everything, paper still plays a powerful role in visual and verbal expression, especially when it's used for masks—the wearable art.

ACTING 101

Masks intrigue kids because they hide and transform at the same time. Like puppets, masks protect the actor from exposure and seem to have a liberating effect, especially on the tongue. Many shy kids become talkative, humorous, and very dramatic when wearing a false face. They come out of hiding when their true identity is camouflaged.

Masks encourage linguistic, interpersonal, and intrapersonal growth. Disguised as animals, villains, heroes, or monsters, kids create characters, construct dialogue, and express a wide range of emotions. So don't wait for Halloween to break out the cover-ups.

PAPER, PAPER EVERYWHERE

Paper's an excellent mask material because it's malleable and accepts attachments easily. It's also plentiful, cheap, or free. Think recycling and you're home free. For starters, gather up shopping bags, paper plates, large envelopes, wrapping paper, newspaper, construction paper, advertising fly-ers, and magazines. Cereal boxes also make a great foundation for a mask. Just add scissors, glue, tape, staplers, marking pens, and imagination.

FIVE-MINUTE MASKS

A pair of sunglasses or goggles becomes a simple mask when bits of paper, feathers, sequins, or yarn are added. Make dog or cat masks starting with paper industrial masks used to filter out dust or paint fumes. Add pipe cleaner whiskers and a tongue. Other instant masks can be made from skin diving, hockey, or ski masks embellished with hats or wigs.

PAPER PLATE MASKS

Take a paper plate and cut a wedge-shaped notch out of the bottom of the fluted rim. Overlap the two edges of the notch and staple together to make a chin. Draw a nose and cut around the bottom and sides, making a flap. Draw the features with crayons or marking pens. Fasten the mask with elas-tic or two ribbons tied around the head.

PAPER BAG MASKS

Giant shopping bag masks are fun because kids can really hide inside. These full-body masks encourage the use of kinesthetic and spatial intelligence because they require larger gestures and more dramatic movement to bring them to life. Shopping-bag-clad children often break into spontaneous dances, twirl, hop, or flap their arms to animate their character.

Make each bag sit all the way down on the head by trimming it to fit around the shoulders or fringing the bottom. Cut wide eyeholes so kids can move safely and a big mouth for easy breathing. Then let kids add earrings, hair, glasses, eyelashes and eyebrows, freckles and rosy cheeks. Try pipe cleaners, yarn, paper strips, curling ribbon, cotton, steel wool, or string. Cut ears, lips, teeth, and eyebrows out of a magazine to make a collage face. Add a variety of hats—baseball, fireman, feathered—to define the characters.

TWO-FACED MASKS

Follow the directions for the paper bag mask but create two characters in one by making a different face on the front and back of the bag. Kids can rotate the mask to play the wolf and the little pig or the sun and the moon. Making one face good and one bad lets them act out opposite emotions in rapid succession or even have a dialogue with themselves playing both parts, tapping into their intrapersonal intelligence.

CARDBOARD MASKS

An oatmeal box makes a wonderful mask for a Tin Man, robot, or Frankenstein monster. Cut the bottom out of the box so you have a cylinder, then slit the box open down the back. Cut out eyeholes and a generous mouth, then attach ears, nose, and eyebrows. The top can be covered with a wig or hat. Cover with foil for the Tin Man. Add bolts to the neck, plus scars and stitches for a monster, or add wires, bulbs, buttons, and batteries to make a robot. This mask can be recycled over and over.

THE ACTOR'S CRAFT

For tips on acting, writing, and staging plays, turn to the sections "The Play's the Thing," in chapter 6, and "Puppets," in this chapter.

THREADNEEDLE STREET

Most kids love to sew—even boys. They start with a swath of limp fabric and end up with anything from a pillow to a pencil case. The best part is crowing, "I made it myself!"

A STITCH IN TIME

Pushing a needle and thread taps directly into kinesthetic intelligence, building eye-hand coordination and fine motor skills. It stimulates mental growth as well, particularly logical and spatial intelligence. To transform a flat plane into a three-dimensional object, needlesmiths have to study the pieces, visualize a final product, then figure out the logical sequence of putting it together, step by step.

As they snip and stitch, they'll tangle with mathematical questions like

How many pieces do I need to make a cube?
How much material will it take to cover this pillow?
How many four-inch circles can I cut out of this scrap?
How big does a pocket need to be to hold a wallet?
What's the least number of seams I'll need to sew this elephant?

In addition, hand sewing develops patience, persistence, and focus. Kids need to be calm and centered as they guide their fingers through the slow, rhythmic process of making an object, stitch by stitch. Kids with strong intrapersonal skills often enjoy the solitary aspect of sewing, which satisfies their creative and introspective impulses at the same time. And finally there's the joy of creative expression, combining colors, patterns, and textures into their own unique designs.

SOURCES OF CLOTH

Cloth is a pleasure in itself, especially for children who favor their visual and kinesthetic intelligences. They can spend hours just looking at the colors, feeling the textures, and mixing and matching fabrics. So when you go looking for cloth, be sure to include your kids in the hunt.

Cloth is almost as plentiful as paper if you recycle what's around your house. Start in the linen closet. No doubt you'll find tablecloths, pillowcases, napkins, and towels that are stained or raggedy, but still usable. Recycle old clothes. A torn blouse can be transformed into a pillow. Two shirt pockets stitched together can surround a scoop of potpourri. Look for cloth at tag and rummage sales, thrift stores, or flea markets. Don't forget the remnant bin at your local fabric store. It's usually overflowing with samples at reduced prices. While you're there pick up thread, needles with large eyes, small scissors, and some straight pins with the colored plastic heads so you can see them before you step on them.

BATH MITT

This is a great no-fail project for first-timers. Kids choose their favorite washcloth—new or used—then fold it over once so it's long and narrow. They sew up the top and side with overhand stitches that are close together. Then they turn it inside out, slip it over their hand, and scrub away. For special effects, a little loofa sponge can be sewn to one side so the mitt is both smooth and rough.

MEMORIES TO LEAN ON

Sentimental kids cling to favorite clothes long after they've outgrown them: "I wore that sweater to preschool." They have precious memories bound up in the sight, feel, and even the smell of old clothes. Woe unto the parent who cleans the closet without checking first. But don't bury old clothes in a drawer. Teach your kids to stitch up a memory pillow.

Kids can take a treasured shirt or sweater and close up the armholes and bottom with a tight overhand stitch. Leave the neck open for stuffing with old nylons or mateless socks, T-shirts with holes, foam rubber, or quilt batting. Sew the neck shut and use the pillow at bedtime or for a cozy reading corner.

POTPOURRI POCKET

Fragrant potpourri bags are popular additions to drawers, trunks, and closets, and they're so simple to make. Take a handkerchief or a patch of thin cloth. Put a scoop of potpourri in the center and tie it closed with a ribbon. Or sew the sides closed to form a pouch. Department stores and bath and gift shops sell potpourri in a staggering array of fragrances. If you have your own garden see the recipes for potpourri in the sections "Heart and Hand," in chapter 9, and "Permanent Pleasures," in chapter 11.

SLEEP PILLOW

A sleep pillow is a fragrance-filled pocket that eases you to sleep and keeps you there. Start with a handkerchief or a piece of soft cloth about that size. Follow the directions for the bath mitt, folding it over, then sewing up the long side and one end. Fill it with a combination of rosemary leaves and lavender blossoms. You can buy both at the herb stand of a farmers' market or in a health food store. Try any fragrance that helps kids relax, such as cinnamon, dried citrus peels, rose petals, or pine needles. Kids can stitch these pillows up as gifts or just to make their own bedtime more inviting.

SOCK DOLLS

A sock doll is a great project for needle-jockeys who want to experiment with yarn and embroidery. This multistep project provides a stiff workout for both spatial and logical intelligences because kids are transforming a simple sock into a complex human form. They'll need one pair of socks for each doll. Use baby socks for a doll just inches high or knee-highs for a lanky one.

1. First stuff the toe of the sock, then tie it off to make the doll's head and neck. Stuff the foot to make the body, with the heel as the buttocks. Sew across the bottom of the body to hold the stuffing in while you make the legs.

2. Now smooth the cuff of the sock and cut it up the middle to form two legs. Sew up the inside of the legs, then gently stuff them using a pencil or chopstick to compact the stuffing. Sew the feet closed. You can use extra stitches to make the toes.

3. Cut the cuff off the second sock and cut it up the middle to form two arms. Stitch the long sides and across one end to make the hands, adding extra stitches to outline the fingers. Then stuff the arms and attach them to the body at the shoulder.

4. Use buttons, marking pens, or embroidery thread to make eyes, nose, and mouth. Yarn can be glued or sewn on for hair. Use another sock, a coffee filter, or a cupcake paper to fashion a hat. Clothing can be made from handkerchiefs, socks, tights, washcloths, remnants, or old baby clothes.

STUFFED ANIMALS

Felt is the best material for animals because it has clean edges that won't unravel. Suggest that kids make a paper pattern of an animal in profile. Good subjects include elephants, pigs, camels, ladybugs, birds, and fish. More confident artists can draw directly on the cloth with chalk. Cut out two pieces exactly alike. Decorate them before they're sewn together—button eyes, thread or pipe-cleaner whiskers, felt or fur ears. Sew the two pieces together around the edges with overhand stitches. Leave a two- or three-inch opening for stuffing. Fill the critter with rags, nylons, foam rubber, quilt batting, or old socks. Use a pencil or chopstick to poke the stuffing into all the corners, then stitch up the opening.

I SPY

If any of the grown-ups in your family wear glasses, they'll appreciate this silky spectacle case. Handy kids can make these gifts in about thirty minutes, so it's a great rainy day activity. And remember that gift giving helps kids feel connected and important to the people around them, reinforcing their interpersonal intelligence.

Search your closets for old ties or drop by a thrift store and look for pretty patterns. Then, cut an eight-inch length off the wide end of the tie, not counting the pointy part at the end. To make the bottom of the case, tuck in about half an inch of the square end and stitch it shut with tiny overhand stitches. Finally, fold down the triangle end and fasten it with Velcro dots or a snap. All done!

DRAFT ANIMAL

Keeping the cold air from sneaking under the door in winter is easy if you have a cozy draft animal. This is just a long tube of cloth, like a jumbo snake, stuffed full of rags, cotton, socks, or batting. Cut a piece of cloth about one yard long and twelve inches wide. Fold it in half and sew the long side shut. Stuff it from each end, using a ruler to push the stuffing in. Sew each end shut. Push it against the foot of the door and the wind will have to find another house to haunt.

PATTERNS

We've all seen parents driven to distraction by questions. Their young tormentors—neither dense nor provocative—are simply trying to understand their world. Questions are the dialect of the growing brain. When kids see a new object, their brains run through a series of questions including *Is this like anything I've already seen?* If so, it fits a category or pattern that supplies a lot of information, instantly. Patterns let kids think in shorthand.

PATTERN PLAY

Being able to spot patterns is a major function of logical intelligence. Kids who are sensitive to patterns have an advantage when they need to analyze, sequence, follow rules, compute, solve problems, see relationships, or reason abstractly. If that sounds like math, you're right. Patterns are the language of math.

EVERYDAY PATTERNS

Pattern practice starts at home. Let little kids help sort and organize the canned goods in the kitchen. They can spot patterns while sorting laundry, especially socks, or organizing the shelves and drawers in their rooms.

If you commute with kids, you can create visual scavenger hunts using patterns in the traffic. Watching for VWs kept my kids from bugging each other on many a long haul. They'd yell "Herby Green" when they spotted a green VW. Out-of-state is the same concept for older kids who can read the small print on license plates. In both games, whoever spots the most, wins.

FINGER FOOD

Patterns are based on math but they have an irresistible appeal to kids with robust visual and kinesthetic intelligence. You can see kids' hands start to itch at the sight of a bin full of small wooden blocks, colorful tiles, bottlecaps, and bits of junk. Adults are amazed at how long kids, even older ones, will work at creating beautiful, complex patterns. The trick is to find lots of finger food, attractive to the eye and touch. Get a basket or box and fill it with

> buttons (look in Grandma's sewing kit)
> marbles
> ceramic tile samples
> pegs and pegboards
> wooden blocks or tiles
> checkers
> bottle caps
> playing cards
> nuts and bolts
> spools of thread

toothpicks and pebbles
sample paint chips (free at the paint store)
various types of beans

If you've already rejected this as a vacuum-choker and a pain in the neck—wait. You can corral pattern activities in a portable work space such as a TV tray, large box lid, or cookie sheet. The containers can be stored under a bed if kids want to keep their patterns and you need a clean room.

NOW STAND BACK

What happens when you leave kids unchaperoned with a pile of pattern materials? Sometimes they'll start by sorting—creating sets. That's the logical part of the brain showing what it already knows. Then the imagination kicks in and patterns become pictures, abstract designs, rose windows, aerial views of cities, or whole galaxies. Now they've entered the visual realm where sensitivity to the elements of art—line, color, and form—allows kids to express ideas and release emotions without saying a word.

Transfer the best designs into wet plaster or glue them on boards. Then go to the library and find books about Simon Rodia and his amazing Watts Towers, shimmering spires of elaborate patterns made from recycled materials and junk.

TIFFANY & CO.

Speaking of junk, drop by a thrift store and scoop up its junkiest beads. Don't be shy—the gaudier the better! Unstring them and put them in a box with needles, thread, ribbons, or shoestrings—whatever kids need to make their own wearable art. Older relatives are a great source of jewelry. Or you can buy about twelve hundred beads for two dollars at the craft store. Beadwork combines patterns, aesthetics, and fine motor skills.

PUZZLES

Puzzles demand a special kind of pattern recognition. The eye studies an empty space, then looks for a form to fill it. Or it starts with the outline of a piece and searches for the opposite configuration. The thousand-piece jigsaws really separate the amateurs from the champs. Kids who excel in puzzle construction see things that are hidden from the hurried eye. Puzzle making strengthens practical problem-solving skills, including the ability to visualize how a broken object should work and then fix it.

PATTERN BOOKS

There are dozens of delightful books and stories built around a pattern or refrain that even nonreaders quickly master. Here are a few:

It's Too Noisy, by Joanna Cole

The Very Hungry Caterpillar, by Eric Carle

The Three Bears

The Billy Goats Gruff

The Three Little Pigs

More elaborate patterns are found in the plot and dialogue of *The Wizard of Oz,* by L. Frank Baum.

PATTERNS IN NATURE AND ART

Turning kids' eyes to the aesthetics of the natural environment is a deceptively simple gift. Once they get the hang of it, they can find beauty almost anywhere, anytime. An aging building, winter-dead trees, the footprints of a squirrel in the snow all offer delight to the motivated viewer.

> *When I was just a little kid, very small in a high chair, my father brought home a lot of little bathroom tiles of different colors. We played with them like dominoes. Pretty soon we were setting them up in more complicated ways—two white tiles and a blue, two white tiles and a blue. When my mother saw, she said leave the poor child alone. But my father said, "I want to show him what patterns are like and how interesting they are. It's a kind of elementary mathematics."*
>
> *What Do You Care What Other People Think?*
>
> — RICHARD FEYNMAN

Go out on a cloudy day and take some time to scan the sky together. Ask your child: *What do the clouds look like to you?* Look at a tree and ask: *What do the branches remind you of? What shapes can you see? Can you make your body look like that tree?* Point out that there are patterns on leaves, seashells, spiderwebs, and butterflies. Look through art books for paintings that use patterns.

WORD PLAY

Word games, poems, songs, nursery rhymes, even football cheers are built on strong auditory patterns. Reciting them builds reading skills in phonics and word families. Here's a simple rhyming competition: "It" chooses a word (*blue*, for example). All the players name words that rhyme with that word (*few, flew, two, glue*) until they run out of rhymes. The last rhymer wins.

Or choose a letter. Each player makes a sentence in which every word starts with that letter—*Betty bought blueberries by begging beyond Brubaker's bakery.* The longest sentence wins—but the funniest usually gets the applause. If your kids really like word games, be sure to see the section "Stiff Cuffs" in chapter 6.

EIGHT

BOOKWORMS

Getting Smarter in the

World of Words

Visual/Spatial

Verbal/Linguistic

Musical

Kinesthetic

Logical/Mathematical

Interpersonal

Intrapersonal

ONE MORE STORY, PLEASE!

When I was five, I desperately wanted my own library card. But a rule is a rule. In those days you had to sign the application in handwriting. So every night I'd practice loopy scrawls on the telephone message pad until I could produce my first and last names with confidence. Finally, I could get my own books.

But this didn't change the most cherished ritual in our household. Bedtime stories. I don't remember when it began, but my dad was still reading to all of us when I was twelve. We grew up to be voracious readers and his grandkids seem to be addicted, too.

Now you may be thinking, "Oh, yeah, we used to read to the kids, but they're getting too old for that." Or, "If I read aloud they'll get lazy and won't want to read on their own."

That's rubbish. Dangerous rubbish.

Research says that the single greatest predictor that a child will become a good reader is if he or she is read to. This is so simple it's scary. If you want kids to be readers, read to them.

EARWORKS

How soon should you start reading to your kids? As soon as they can be propped up in your lap. And don't stop until they're enrolled in algebra.

Here's why kids get smarter when *you* read to them. Language is ultimately the tool of thought. The more words kids know, the more varied, precise, and rich their thinking can be. As they hear new words in context their vocabulary grows. They internalize a variety of sentence patterns, and that helps them when they speak and write. They learn the forms of literature that they will encounter in school.

Hearing stories about people helps develop interpersonal intelligence. Autobiography, biography, and fictional stories with vivid characters let kids see life from another person's point of view. They learn what motivates people, how others solve problems and deal with the consequences of their actions. Those insights build social skills.

Perhaps most important, kids feel loved because you spend your precious time sharing stories with them. They love books because you do. Need I say more? Don't wait another day. Go to the public library, scoop up a bunch of books, and just start reading together. Here are some tips to jump-start the process.

TIP #1: SHOPPING LISTS OF BOOKS

A library is a big place. Staring at the spines of thousands of books can be daunting. So how do you choose? The children's librarian is your first, best source of suggestions and titles. But you can also do research on your own using any of the following books.

Great Books for Girls, by Kathleen Odean.

More Books Kids Will Sit Still For: A Read-Aloud Guide, by Judy
Freeman.

The Read-Aloud Handbook, by Jim Trelease.

Once upon a Heroine, by Alison Cooper-Mullin.

Black Authors and Illustrators of Children's Books, by Barbara
Rollock.

TIP #2: READ BY AUTHOR

If you read *Charlie and the Chocolate Factory* and hated to reach the last
page, you might want to read all of Roald Dahl's books. If your child wonders where writers get their ideas, Dahl is a perfect author to learn on.
Reading his autobiography, *Boy: Tales of Childhood,* they'll discover that the
witches, candy factory, and pesty kids came from real adventures in his
youth. The dead mouse chapter is great fun.

TIP #3: READ BY THEME

Read books related to your child's latest passion—dragons, robots, castles,
outer space, dinosaurs. Kids build up tremendous stores of information this
way. You're modeling how to do research and turn an interest into an area of
expertise.

TIP #4: READ ABOUT PLACES

Read about destinations. When you're planning a vacation out of state or to
another country, find books set in that region to create interest and suggest
itinerary ideas. Or read books about the region after you get home. It's a
great way to savor your memories, and kids love saying, "I've seen that."

If Grandma and Grandpa live far away, find picture books of their town to build a visual context for phone calls. Children feel closer to relatives if they can "see" where they live instead of just hearing a disembodied voice.

TIP #5: READ TO SHARE A LOVE OF HISTORY

A fascinating way to hook kids on the past is to read time machine books. Most of these stories start in the present with curious kids who unlock the secret to time travel and escape to another century. The young heroes joust with knights, rescue maidens, and learn to adjust to life without TV. Upon their return, they know a lot about history and have a new appreciation for home and family.

Some time machine titles:

MIDDLE AGES

Max and Me and the Time Machine, by Gery Greer.

Happily Ever After, by Anna Quindlen.

Stranger in the Mist, by Paul McCusker.

The Kid Who Got Zapped Through Time, by Deborah Scott.

The Sword of Culann and *The Griffon's Nest,* by Betty Levin.

A Connecticut Yankee in King Arthur's Court, by Mark Twain.

RENAISSANCE

The Trolley to Yesterday, by John Bellairs.

CIVIL WAR

The Root Cellar, by Janet Lunn.

My access to the New York Public Library was what allowed me to pursue my thirst for knowledge. It was there I sought out an education for myself. I'd sit and read, do my homework or browse through the many wonderful books that lined the shelves. The library became my home away from home.

Growing Up in the Sanctuary of My Imagination

— NICHOLASA MOHR

19TH CENTURY

Time Out, by Helen Cresswell.

The Ghost in the Mirror, by John Bellairs.

The Switching Well, by Peni Griffin.

TIP #6: HAVE FUN WHEN YOU READ

First of all, get cozy. Some kids insist on being in your lap, even when their feet almost touch the floor. It can also be fun for them to see your face while you read, especially if you're one of those people who can't tell a story without making faces that bring it to life. When you read, forget yourself. Use silly, gruff, or timid voices to help the characters stand out and to convey emotion. Talk faster at the exciting parts and slower to create drama.

When you turn the page of a picture book, pause and let the illustrations tell the next part of the story. Encourage kids to comment on what they see. Ask: *What's happening now?*

You don't have to read every word. For very young listeners, you can summarize parts of the story or tell it in your own words. However, this won't work with older kids who've memorized the text and want to hear it exactly the same way every time.

Ask questions while you read:

What do you think will happen now?
Why do you think she did that?
How do you think he feels now?
What would you do?

Ask questions after the story:

What part did you like best?
Would you like to have that character for
a friend?

TIP #7: SAVING THOSE MEMORIES

Over the course of a childhood, lucky children hear and read hundreds of books. Later, as adults, they struggle in vain to recall the name of their favorite book. The cover was green, they sobbed at the end, but the title escapes them.

Why not start a simple log in which you record the name of each book you read? You can use a spiral notebook, a scrapbook, or sheets of paper in a folder. You can write the title and your child can make a simple picture to go with it. Later, your child can take over the writing part. Believe me, they'll love looking at this when they're grown up and it can be a starting point for reading to the next generation.

On the couch, in the living room, between his seventh and eighth birthdays, Herbert George Wells discovered reading. Years later he would recall mastering the technique of "leaving my body to sit impassive in a crumpled up attitude in a chair or sofa, while I wandered over the hills and far away in novel company and new scenes." This was magic. He discovered worlds far beyond Atlas House and High Street. . . . Thousands of these worlds all neatly printed and illustrated with the most magnificent pictures.

H. G. Wells

— KEITH FERRELL

READ ALL ABOUT IT

Newspapers are a mystery to kids. Why do adults pore over them like the Rosetta stone in the morning and yell if they're not in the trash by nightfall? Why is the page so big and the print so small? Like most kids, I never got beyond the funnies until middle school. Yet newspapers are perfect tools for helping kids as young as five learn to read and write.

NEWSPRINT FOR PRE-READERS

Let's start with the alphabet. Little kids get very excited when they begin to recognize their letters. Unfortunately, some well-meaning parents rush out and buy workbooks or flashcards. Most of these "learning aids" are about as interesting as watching paint dry. Kids either lose interest or rebel, and that's not a great start for a lifelong reading plan. On the other hand, for no money at all your child can frolic with hundreds of letters in their natural habitat—the words and paragraphs of the front page.

A newspaper has every letter of the alphabet in dozens of sizes, type-faces, and colors. Stick a marking pen in your child's hand and let her circle every *A* or *Z* she sees. That's fun! She can move on from letters to little words. Soon she'll be asking, *What does this say?* and she's on her way to reading.

RANSOM READERS

Snipping jumbo letters from sale pages and headlines is a great way to start an alphabet book. Kids can stick the letter **A** on a blank page and then draw or cut out pictures of things that start with **A**. Working their way through the alphabet becomes a personal phonics program.

Learning to spell is more fun with the ransom reader approach because it stimulates both visual and kinesthetic intelligence. Kids can cut heaps of letters from the newspaper and use them like Scrabble tiles to spell first words, like the names of family members, pets, or favorite foods. Kids remember words more easily when spelling is a hands-on, graphic design activity.

A THOUSAND WORDS

Our world is saturated with pictures that even toddlers can speed-read, especially commercial images like McDonald's golden arches. Learning to "read" pictures in the newspaper can help your child in school, where many literature and social studies lessons begin by discussing an illustration. Charts and graphs in math lessons are another type of picture reading that kids must master to succeed in school, so plunging into the newspaper several time a week can be as educational as a dose of homework and much more interesting.

To encourage news-picture literacy, give your kids a scrapbook or loose-leaf binder so they can start a collection of interesting photos. As they browse through their pictures, ask:

Who do you think these people are?
Where do you think they are?
What are they doing?
How do you think they feel?
How can you tell?

They can also create art work by combining images into a collage. If the pictures are black-and-white, they can be hand-colored like old photographs with colored pencils, watercolors, crayons, or chalk.

EDITOR-IN-CHIEF

Give most kids a pen and the front page and suddenly it's mustache season. Every face is sprouting. You can stimulate linguistic intelligence by giving that editorial impulse a nudge. Show kids how to draw speech bubbles like cartoon artists use and ask them to fill in what the people in the pictures might be saying. Or erase the words in their favorite comic strip. The ink lifts off easily with a soft eraser and then they can make up their own stories.

WEATHER OR NOT

Monitoring the weather page is a great way to stimulate mathematical intelligence and build geography awareness. Young kids can read the symbols on weather maps—snowflakes and zigzags of lightning. Older kids love extremes—"No way! A hundred and fifteen in Dallas!"—so let them scan the columns for the scorchers and freezers. Checking the global charts is a painless introduction to foreign capitals and a good way to compare seasons and weather around the world.

Make a weather scavenger hunt by asking how much rain Grandma got yesterday. *How cold is it at your cousins' house? How many places will be over one hundred today?* The weather section is practical, too. Before heading off on vacation, have the kids check the high and low temperatures of your destination to decide if you should pack sweaters or sunblock.

SPORTS CONNECTION

In some families, the most important item on the breakfast table is the sports section. It's not the twenty-four-hour sports channel, but kids can get hooked on the photographs, headlines, and statistics of their heroes.

Next time you trek out to the stadium, point out the press box. Then check the paper the next morning to see how the reporter described the game. Some sports writers have a real talent for capturing the humor and humanity of sports. If you have a sports nut, you won't have to mention more than once the idea of cutting out pictures of heroes for a bulletin board or collage.

ENTERTAINMENT

I knew a family where the kids couldn't watch television until they checked the listings in the paper. If the "pickin's" were slim, Mom would suggest another activity. Meanwhile the kids learned a lot about reading timetables and program summaries. The only surfing they did was at the beach.

> *One day I noticed Danny Freeman, then in fourth grade, sitting at the dining table and casually reading the newspaper. I was hugely impressed. Wow! I became aware of my first ambition in life. I yearned to be able to read a newspaper.*
>
> *The Abracadabra Kid*
>
> — SID FLEISCHMAN

LET YOUR FINGERS DO THE SHOPPING

For many kids, a refrigerator is like a home shopping channel. They open the door, gaze and graze, then wander off, satisfied. Next visit, the shelves are miraculously full again. They'll never appreciate the shopping and schlepping it takes to keep the larder stocked until they're involved in the process.

So put them to work as Menu Consultants. Pull out the weekly food section, arm them with paper, pencil, scissors, highlighter, whatever they need for menu planning. As they cruise the food ads, they'll build practical math skills by comparing prices, noticing sale items, and computing coupon savings. They'll appreciate you and mealtime more if they participate.

GETTING AN EARFUL

School's a tough place for kids who don't hear well. Not the ones with impaired hearing. I mean kids who learn best with their eyes and hands—visual and kinesthetic learners. Even simple classes require ears "on steroids." Take a look at the auditory hurdles first-graders face when a teacher gets rolling:

1. Can they scoop up all the words, even if the teacher's back is turned?

2. Can they maintain their focus as invisible information floods their auditory pathways?

3. Can they make sense of the information as the lesson rolls along?

4. Can they store auditory information successfully for later use?

5. Can they do it all at once, and quickly?

Only the sharpest ears survive.

THE EIGHTEEN-YEAR CONVERSATION

So what can you do to give your kids the ear muscle they need to succeed in school? Talk, talk, talk. Do it when they're little. Do it when they're big. Do it when they're fascinated. Do it when they're bored. And when you get tired of talking, find other ways to bathe your kids in rich, vivid language.

Here's why:

⇛ Auditory skills take a long time to develop. The language pathways in the brain are not completely mature until adolescence or even later, so listening is the most difficult way for young children to absorb information.

⇛ Weak auditory skills get stronger with practice.

⇛ Proficiency and pleasure in reading and writing grow primarily through listening and speaking.

MORE ABOUT CONVERSATIONS

My parents taught us to talk the old-fashioned way—at dinnertime. There were seven of us around the table, all vying for center stage. My brother David complained that if he stopped to eat, he'd lose his place. My dad joked that he couldn't get a word in edgewise. We adored these nightly gabfests and we're still talking—I've got the phone bills to prove it.

So make your home a talking place. Avoid yelling and silence, since both interfere with language growth. Don't frighten children into being cautious and hesitant. Don't equate silence with virtue. Kids need to play with language, freely and clumsily, just as they must teeter, stumble, and fall when they're learning to walk. Make room for kids in adult conversations. Ask them to share their ideas on how to solve problems. Be sure to listen attentively and take their ideas seriously. If you have lively discussions and use a rich vocabulary, they'll copy you. That's how language works.

READING

The section "One More Story, Please!" earlier in this chapter urges you to read to your kids. Be sure to check that section again because there's really no substitute for hearing good literature on a warm lap. That noisy bunch

161

of kids at my mom's table fell silent the minute my dad settled down to read to us each night. Even at the age of twelve, it was still the highlight of my day.

AUDIOTAPES

Of course, some children are insatiable for stories and it's damned near impossible to read aloud while changing freeway lanes or carving a pot roast. So stick a cassette in the tape deck and kill two birds with one story. You'll get some well-deserved peace while your kids work on auditory processing skills, painlessly, happily, quietly.

Story tapes are excellent tools for building vocabulary, attention span, and comprehension. Without actual pictures, kids have to think about the words and try to see the story in their heads. This technique of visualizing also strengthens memory and can improve spelling.

Finally, story tapes provide excellent language models. Listening to the dramatic, fluent voice of a storyteller helps kids become more expressive readers and speakers.

ALL TYPES OF TAPES

There's a wide range of literature available on tape at your library or bookstore. Don't be afraid of classics like *The Wind in the Willows* or *The Wizard of Oz.* The text may be a bit of a stretch for younger kids but the story will seduce them. As they listen, they'll internalize basic story structures—plot, character, setting, and action—which helps when writing stories of their own.

➻ Nonfiction tapes on science, history, the environment, or famous people are an excellent way to teach kids lots of information effortlessly.

➤→ Poetry tapes introduce kids to the imaginative use of language. They learn to recognize rhyming and anticipate patterns in language. For example, children easily memorize Mother Goose because of the strong rhyming structure, like a drumbeat.

➤→ Music tapes that embed information in songs are another painless form of learning. The music locks the information in the memory. Just humming a few notes brings it all back. How else can we explain the way very young kids sing the whole alphabet before they ever know what a Z is? Mr. Rogers croons at least half of his messages to his audience. If your child has trouble spelling a word, try putting the letters to a simple tune, like "Old MacDonald."

SOURCES OF TAPES

The children's section of your public library probably has a broad selection of story tapes. Look for plastic bags that hold a tape with a companion book.

If you can't face *Green Eggs and Ham* one more time, read it into a tape recorder and your child can have Dr. Seuss room service for breakfast, lunch, and dinner.

Have a grandparent or uncle read stories into a tape recorder so you can start your own library of family storytellers on tape.

Set up a tape-trading club and encourage kids to swap with friends. Just put a piece of masking tape with your name on the cassettes for easy identification.

A LIBRARY CARD

Libraries are smorgasbords for the mind. All you can read. Every day. Free. Kids are amazed that they can check out more books than they can carry. You'll be amazed at how many different intelligences flourish between the covers of a book.

If you want to create avid library patrons in your family, use these strategies for successful book trips. First, give kids a snack before your visit. Hungry kids can't focus on books. When you arrive, don't dawdle at the new fiction shelves. Head straight for the children's section where short furniture, bright books, and multicolored computers announce that this is a playground for young brains.

DOWN MEMORY LANE

You can nurture interpersonal and intrapersonal intelligence through the simple act of sharing some of the stories that you loved as a child. Go to the shelves and find one of your favorite childhood books. Many of the classics like *The Little House on the Prairie* or *The Wind in the Willows,* are still favorites with young readers. Sit and read part of the book together and talk about why you loved it. Then ask your child to share a favorite book. Or just wander and browse together. Do your kids have a current passion? Type it into the computer catalog or ask the librarian to help you track down books on the subject.

Don't stop with the local branch. Find a big old library with all the trimmings. These architectural wonders have music rooms, ceiling murals, and cases and cases of very old children's books that you can sample. Just don't stay too long. Build the library habit with frequent short visits.

MEET THE EXPERT

The children's librarian is a fount of knowledge. Introduce your kids through a question: *Where are the dinosaur books? How can I learn about penguins? How many books did Sid Fleischman write?*

Shy kids warm up once they realize that librarians love kids who love books. As they build a relationship with the resident book expert, your children will pick up valuable skills that will help them when they're doing book reports, research papers, and projects.

BROWSING

How do you choose your books? By cover, title, author, first sentence, typeface, or instinct? Do you use the catalog or just strafe the shelf with your eyes? Kids need to find their own method by browsing. So when you follow your kids to the children's section, bring a book for yourself and relax while they comb the collection. Kids with strong visual leanings may pore over the pictures. The linguistically inclined may sample the text, starting from the middle or jumping from back to front. Most kids make piles and change their minds. Try not to rush them or tell them the right way to choose. Browsing is a literacy skill.

RETURNING BOOKS

The downside of borrowing books is the due date. Typically parents have to send out a search party and at least one book is AWOL. Lost books cause fear, guilt, threats and tears (not to mention hefty fines). They spoil an otherwise perfect activity. So here are some tips for keeping track of books between visits:

Printouts

Most libraries are computerized. After you check out, make a quick stop at the clerk's desk and ask for a printout. Weeks later when it's time for the return trip, kids will have a checklist in hand, so gathering up their books is more scavenger hunt than test of memory.

Books on a Leash

Sometimes library books burrow among your possessions and aren't discovered until spring cleaning or an earthquake. A book leash helps kids spot stowaways. Open the front cover of the book. Loop bright-colored yarn or ribbon all the way around the cover from top to bottom. Tie the ends together and let them hang down at the bottom like a tail. It's easy to spot the yarn when the search is on.

Book Basket

Train your kids to dump their finished books in a book basket by the front door. On library day only a few minutes are needed to round up the stragglers.

SUMMER READING PROGRAMS

Most libraries sponsor summertime reading clubs for kids of all ages. The clubs have a theme, activities, a special log, and a final celebration. It can be an incentive to the reluctant reader or a place to meet other book lovers.

ANY QUESTIONS?

Still reluctant to make the book trek? Read on. Children's author Sid Fleischman describes the wonder of falling under the spell of a book in his autobiography, *The Abracadabra Kid.*

> *I was soon turning the pages of Robin Hood and could hear voices. I didn't need audio. I could hear the sharp clash of swords and pikestaffs. I took up residence in Sherwood Forest for a solid year or two, and the experience has never entirely left me. I still can't pass up a discarded wood lath lying in the alley without thinking I could make a splintery sword out of it.*

FAMILY TRADITIONS

Start a birthday tradition. Ask about donating a book to the library with your child's name on a bookplate announcing: TO CELEBRATE HANNAH'S FIFTH BIRTHDAY. She'll run to the shelf every time to see if her birthday book is checked out.

In Topeka, Langston's mother took him regularly to the public library, a small but impressive ivy-covered stone building on the grounds of the state capitol; he was entranced by the bright silence of the reading room, the big chairs, the long smooth tables, the attentive librarians who fetched books at his command. Langston began to believe "in nothing but books and the wonderful world in books— where if people suffered, they suffered in beautiful language, not in monosyllables, as we did in Kansas."

The Life of

Langston Hughes

— ARNOLD RAMPERSAD

NINE

RAINY DAYS AND SUNDAYS

Getting Smarter around the House

Visual /Spatial

Verbal /Linguistic

Musical

Kinesthetic

Logical/Mathematical

Interpersonal

Intrapersonal

POTLUCK

Some adults think cooking with kids inevitably leads to a 911 call—either to douse the flames or to hose down the mess. Cooking doesn't have to be life-threatening or sloppy, if you turn your kitchen into a cooking academy. Go step by step and you could end up with a junior Julia Child.

MIXMASTER 101

There are lots of great cookbooks for kids. This isn't one of them. But the ideas in this section provide simple, no-fail opportunities for the youngest cooks to grow gastronomically and mentally. Cooking is a simple activity that uses most of the brain to get the job done. It starts with a large portion of logical and kinesthetic intelligence, sprinkled with visual, interpersonal, and linguistic skills.

Cooking is aesthetic. It bombards the senses of sight, smell, touch, and taste and has a set of movements that resemble choreography in the finest chefs. At first little kids struggle to simply control hands and bowl, but kinesthetic skills emerge as they practice stirring, kneading, cutting, and pouring.

Food preparation requires discipline. Kids must focus and concentrate. They strain their logic and memory circuits to keep track of where they are in the recipe and what comes next. Schoolwork requires the same skills but rarely tastes as good.

Kids who know how to cook enjoy a sense of self-reliance and confidence. They feel secure knowing they can fend for themselves in the kitchen, and nothing builds egos like pushing the speed limit on a Cuisinart.

FOR STARTERS

Little kids love to imitate adults, so boost your kindergartner up on a stool and start with the basics: smearing, stirring, pouring, and licking the spoon. Be sure to talk, describing and explaining as you cook. Little chefs develop eye-hand coordination, fine motor skills, and kitchen vocabulary following your lead.

↦ Biscuits: These sticky treats from a tube become a whole project when kids decorate them with raisins, cinnamon and sugar, nuts, dried fruit, apple slices, pieces of cheese, or bacon. Be sure kids watch through the oven window as the biscuits rise and brown.

↦ Soup: I loved to crumble Saltine crackers into steaming tomato soup until it looked like light pink oatmeal. Canned soup is a quick dish that begs to be improved. Ask your kids: *What could we add that would make this taste better?* Some possibilities: canned corn, chunks of cheese, croutons, finely chopped fresh vegetables, slices of sausage, crumbled bacon, dried herbs, yogurt.

↦ Things on toast: Toast is perfect for little hands. It's rough and noisy and it stands up to a knife. Let them smear it with honey, peanut butter, jam, or cream cheese, or add grated cheese or colored sprinkles. If you want to get fancy, give kids cookie cutters to press shapes out of fresh bread, then toast and top.

↪   Desserts: Jell-O, tapioca, and puddings just require stirring and waiting. They test the limits of delayed gratification for most youngsters, especially if the pudding is chocolate. Licking the spoon helps.

↪   Sun tea: Start with a big jar of water, dangle three or four tea bags in and set it in the sun for six hours. Add mint leaves, lemon or orange slices, strawberries or cloves. This is a sweet activity for a summer morning.

GRADE-SCHOOL GOURMETS

Once kids have some experience handling bowls, spoons, and sifters, they're ready for more responsibility and less direction. If they can read, measure, and mix, buy an apron with big pockets, tie it around yourself, shove your hands deep in the pockets, and keep them there. Say over and over to yourself, **Do nothing for kids that they can do for themselves.** The kitchen's a safe place for kids to make decisions and learn from mistakes, so try to stay in the background.

When older kids cook, they're exploring the practical application of mathematical intelligence: quantity, measuring, approximation, equivalents, and temperature. Cooking also develops linguistic intelligence because recipes require careful reading and excellent comprehension. Following a recipe for banana bread sharpens skills that novels never touch. Once kids get a taste of their first culinary triumph, they'll dive back into the cookbooks for more. That's literacy in action.

↪   Batter breads—corn, banana, and pumpkin—improve with some additions. Kids can experiment with raisins, nuts, canned corn, cranberries, dried fruit, currants, and sunflower seeds. This might be the time to start a cooking journal to record their original ideas.

↪ Biscuits from scratch are fun, especially if kids add cheese, nuts, raisins, or spices to the mix. Or make a fingerprint in the center of the raw biscuit and add a dollop of jam before baking.

↪ Cookies of all kinds are favorite projects. Snickerdoodles were my favorites because we rolled them into balls, then rolled the balls in cinnamon and sugar. Peanut butter for the crisscrossing with the fork. And of course chocolate chip, so kids can prospect for chips in the raw dough.

↪ Scrambled eggs can be made tastier with additions including cheese, bacon, mushrooms, onions, asparagus, pimentos, olives, sour cream, salsa, or herbs.

↪ Layered dishes are more construction than cooking and require no heat or sharp knives. A favorite is bean dip. Layer refried beans, sour cream, shredded cheese, pitted olives, avocado, and chopped tomatoes or salsa. Chill and serve with chips. Put it out at parties and watch it disappear.

↪ Soup from scratch, especially on a rainy day, is a great project for older kids. Start with prepared broth or boil up some bones and bouillon. When the broth has some body, start adding. Canned or frozen vegetables work, but chopping fresh vegetables is more satisfying. Encourage kids to try out some dried herbs and spices—a little at a time until their taste buds applaud.

↪ Smoothies are healthy drinks that kids mistakenly adore. Take ice, yogurt, fruit juice, and bananas, strawberries, or other ripe fruit and throw it all in a blender. Hold your ears, and one minute later your mouth will be in heaven. Of course, adults should supervise closely whenever electric appliances are used.

➼ Shish kebabs appeal because of the poking and the patterns. For snacks, kids can skewer fresh fruit and marshmallows and serve with a yogurt-honey dipping sauce. Or try vegetable kebabs drizzled with salad dressing. A plastic knife is tough enough for most jobs so you don't need to worry if you're supervising a group.

➼ Egg salad is a cinch to make, since hard-boiled eggs yield to a fork or pastry cutter. Just add relish, mustard, mayonnaise, and a dash of salt and pepper.

KITCHEN CHEMISTRY

Most people agree that the difference between a good cook and a gifted chef is imagination. Culinary explorers taste and stir their way through a menu guided by the question, *"I wonder what would happen if . . . ?"* Young chefs exercise their creativity by combining ingredients that make most adults lunge for the Rolaids. But it's their invention and they'll devour it. Who do you suppose thought of peanut butter and bananas? Experimenting with cooking methods is a great way for kids to observe the effects of heat— direct flame, the toaster oven, and a double boiler all produce specific effects. Heat management is a major accomplishment that requires patience and close supervision. Expect some scorched chocolate pudding along the way.

BOOKS ABOUT COOKS

Many kids who hate to read love to read cookbooks. There are shelves and shelves of them in the children's section of the public library. Used book stores are another great source for cook-books and food magazines. You can also settle down together with a homemade snack and a novel about food. You read aloud or take turns between bites.

> *Much Ado about Aldo, Aldo Applesauce, Aldo Ice Cream,* and *Aldo Peanut Butter,* by Johanna Hurwitz. These books are about Aldo, age eight, who decides to give up eating meat.

> *Justin and the Best Biscuits in the World,* by Mildred Walter. Justin visits his grandfather's ranch and discovers that housework is for boys, too.

> *Burgoo Stew,* by Susan Patron. Billy uses a secret ingredient and a little kindness to tame a bunch of rough, hungry boys.

A PICTURE IS WORTH A THOUSAND WORDS

As I munched, thirty-five or forty years rolled back. . . . A flood of clear and distinct memories that had been locked away became immedi-ate and accessible. The meaningless suburban highway transformed, became a street with streetcars. The next errant breeze might carry the sound of distant cheering at Wrigley Field or the redolence of the stockyards.

As heard on *All Things Considered,* April 16, 1993
— DANIEL PINKWATER, on discovering authentic Chicago hot dogs in Poughkeepsie

On Saturday morning, I love to pour a second cup of coffee, sit at the kitchen counter, and watch cooking shows with my son Anthony. These programs are a great way for visual and auditory learners to pick up techniques and some terrific recipes. Check your public television station or the cooking channel. You can also rent cooking tapes from the library.

Our local farmers' market has cooking demonstrations every Saturday. We've also found wonderful, inexpensive cooking classes at the local adult school. *Bon appétit!*

HEART AND HAND

Kids are never too young to practice the art of giving by making simple gifts for family and friends. Nothing fancy or expensive. Intention and action—heart and hand—are the essential elements. When kids focus on pleasing others, the benefits flow in both directions. While they're lifting spirits, they get a boost right in their self-esteem. Kids who give feel valuable.

Gift making also strengthens kinesthetic, visual, and logical intelligence. Homemade projects typically require kids to focus not only their eyes and hands but their minds, as they follow step by step from idea through construction. Parents are often astonished at how long wiggly kids can concentrate on creative projects.

NOSE GIFTS

Kids can make fragrant gifts that go back to the Middle Ages, when times were tough for sensitive nostrils. With no sewers, showers, or garbage collection, stink was the order of the day. So people found clever ways to relieve the nasal assault.

POMANDERS

Pomanders are fragrant globes of citrus and cloves that people held under their noses as they picked their way through smelly streets. Kids as young as five can make pomanders for seasonal giving.

First, choose a firm lemon, orange, or grapefruit. Give kids a nail and have them prick holes in the fruit, then push cloves into the holes until only the star-shaped heads show. They can make circular or diamond patterns. This activity develops the kinesthetic ability to manipulate small objects skillfully. Kids learn focus and patience because the fruit needs to be completely covered with cloves. When all the poking's done, dust the fruit with cinnamon. Tie a ribbon around it and set it aside to dry for one to two weeks. Pomanders are great in drawers or hung in closets.

POTPOURRI

Long ago this mix of fruit and flowers freshened the air in rooms that never saw sunlight or a mop. To make your own potpourri, lay flower petals and strips of citrus peel on a cookie sheet and put it in a warm, dry place such as an attic, a water heater closet, or an oven with a pilot light. When the mix is dry, blend in some cloves, allspice, nutmeg, or cinnamon bark. Store it all in a jar for a few weeks, then put a scoopful in a piece of thin cloth and tie with a ribbon. These packets are lovely to tuck in drawers or to keep in cars that have lost their showroom smell.

ORNAMENTAL SCENTS

Cinnamon ornaments can decorate a holiday tree or perfume a closet all year. First, kids mix up a simple dough, combining one-third cup of cinnamon, one-third cup of flour, and two-thirds cup of applesauce. Roll it out like pie dough. If it's sticky, add more cinnamon, not flour. Cut the dough with a cookie cutter. Poke a hole in each ornament and let it dry on a rack for two days. Thread a ribbon through the hole and the ornament is ready to hang. Put a half dozen in a bag for a wonderful gift.

WRAPPING EDIBLE GIFTS

Summer gardens usually produce too much of a good thing, so share the wealth by letting your kids deliver gifts from the garden. But how do you wrap zucchini? Decorate brown bags with drawings, stickers, or sponge-paint designs. Insert veggies and tie with raffia, lace, or ribbon. Give a strawberry basket the treatment by weaving ivy in and out, sticking flowers through the holes, or tying ribbons to each corner. Fill it with tomatoes, apricots, or plums for some lucky neighbor.

There are dozens of easy cookie recipes that kids follow with very little help. When the cookies are cool, layer them in old tin boxes or tiny baskets. Decorated bags tied with ribbon make cheerful containers, or a big coffee mug can hold a half dozen cookies for break time.

Choosing recipients, delivering gifts, and accepting thank-yous gracefully all develop interpersonal intelligence. When all the gifting is done, be sure to talk with your child about how it feels to share with others.

ARTISTS AND WRITERS

Note cards are useful gifts that announce the artist in your child. You can buy blank note cards and matching envelopes at discount paper stores. Give your kids a set of marking pens and a few ideas—holiday cards, birthday cards, abstract designs, landscapes, or animals. Or they can glue on dried flowers or leaves for nature designs. See the section "Permanent Pleasures" in chapter 11 for directions. A half-dozen cards with envelopes fit snugly in a Baggie. With a bit of ribbon, this is a gift that kids of all ages can give with pride.

MUSIC TAPES

If your child plays a musical instrument well, make a tape recording of a miniconcert and send it along to grandparents, cousins, aunts, and uncles.

GARDEN IN A JAR

Kids should recycle an old fishbowl or stout mason jar for this micro-jungle. Put a layer of pebbles on the bottom of the jar, then a layer of potting soil or dirt. Insert small plants or cuttings and add water, but not enough to make the soil soggy. Cover the opening with plastic wrap and find a sunny place. Raindrops will collect at the top and recycle. When the balance is right, this terrarium is a zero-maintenance gift.

AT THE TABLE

Kids can make clever napkin rings with buttons. These are especially good for a holiday table. Simply sort through your button collection for interesting shapes and colors. Thread about twelve buttons on a pipe cleaner or piece of elastic about six inches long. Push the buttons close together and twist or tie the ends of the pipe cleaner or elastic. Kids can personalize the rings by painting initials on the buttons. Thread paper or cloth napkins through the rings, then pile them in a basket for giving.

BOARD GAMES

It's been decades since I spent a rainy afternoon lost in the world of dice and spinners. But I distinctly remember Monopoly marathons, during which my siblings and I barely stopped for meals. We adored the competition, but the best part was sprawling around the board, teasing, laughing, and occasionally going to jail.

Board games like Monopoly are a refuge for kids who are duffers on the playing field, where size and grit rule. In contrast, board games involve a fair amount of luck, so muscular, smart, or agile kids have an equal shot at last place. Despite the element of chance, board games actually sharpen dozens of skills.

THE BRAIN GAIN

↦   Spatial intelligence: Board games develop visual flexibility. Kids learn to see in various dimensions and directions, picturing the board in reverse, keeping track of their opponents' pieces and their own all at once.

↦   Strategic thinking: Good players exercise their logical intelligence by planning a series of moves and then visualizing the whole sequence. It's like playing the game with no hands. This if/then thinking is useful in the real world and a game board is a safe place to practice.

↦   Advance planning: Thinking of strategies isn't enough. The great players weigh the value of various strategies, looking at both short-term and long-term gains. Kids may learn to sacrifice one piece to lure an opponent into a more advantageous scheme. Eventually they may apply that thinking to the game of life, where you let opponents win on some points so you can win others.

⇥ Interpersonal intelligence: Board games help kids learn valuable social skills. They learn to take turns, even when it means watching someone destroy their brilliant plans. They learn to read their opponents and anticipate their next move.

⇥ Emotional growth: Good sports are kids with a lot of intrapersonal intelligence. They've learned the value of emotional control. When they see their success wiped out by a roll of the dice, they have to remain calm and improvise solutions. The lesson they're learning is to deal with disappointment and recover. Kids can practice both winning and losing gracefully once they understand that a victory doesn't mean one person is better than the other.

THE TRICK OF IT

Most board games are based on a simple principle: getting from start to finish first. Players move along a path, prompted by cards, dice, or spinners. One variation involves acquiring the most of something along the way. Hundreds of commercial games are built on these simple formats. With that knowledge in hand, kids can design dozens of their own games.

HOMEMADE BOARD GAMES

Kids are intrigued by the idea of creating a miniworld that runs on their rules. Making the board is easy. They just need a sturdy piece of cardboard and some marking pens.

181

The first task is to find a theme for the game. It can be saving the environment, adventures in the rain forest, traveling through time, prehistoric life, cyberspace, and so on. The theme determines the world of the game—activities, illustrations, conflicts, villains, and heroes. Linguistic intelligence and imagination are the main ingredients.

Once they've identified the world of their game, kids start thinking technically: *How many players? What's the goal? How will the pieces move? One die or two? What will the cards say?*

At this point their logic and language circuits will get a good workout. Writing directions is a lot harder than it looks, so the game may go through several drafts before it's ready for a road test. As kids play the first round, problems usually arise and they're back to the drawing board. More thinking required.

MORE TIPS FOR DESIGNERS

➥ Design a basic board, with start, finish, and a pathway between. Then make up several games with different themes, cards, and rules. They can all be played on the same board.

➥ Hook two or more boards together to create a mega-game where the rules are blended or change from one section to another, rather like driving across state lines.

➥ Designers with strong spatial intelligence may want to try a three-dimensional board. Most commercial games are flat because it makes them easy to package and store. But do-it-yourself designers can invent 3-D boards with aerial paths like bridges, ladders, staircases, freeway off-ramps and elevated subway lines.

COMMERCIAL GAMES

There are hundreds of commercial games that stimulate young minds, but chess and Monopoly are at the head of the class.

CHESS is touted as a game of strategy that teaches kids to think ahead, make plans, and consider a variety of options. There's also a strong social element in chess: Hierarchy + Opportunity = Power. Kids are acutely aware of power and privilege, since they generally have little of either. The chess pieces act a lot like people. They play by different rules and approach situations differently—some shyly, some boldly, some when you least expect it. Responding to these situations on the chessboard helps kids adapt in real life.

MONOPOLY is an aerial view of a community and a lesson in socio-economics. In one trip around the board kids learn about public utilities, transportation monopolies, landlords and renters, taxes, charities, and incarceration.

It's like an amusement park for logical learners because it's loaded with practical math. Making change, paying debts, computing real estate values and rental income, comparing values, plotting trading and investment strategies. Plus, there's the constant flow of conversation as reading, debating, and bragging fuel the game.

What else can you learn from Monopoly? My brother Bob, who was the real estate wiz, still is. My brother Rick, who hid money under the board to fake us out, became a lawyer.

PLAYING ALONG

You can learn a lot about how your kids think from observing their home-made games. Pay attention to the logic and complexity of the rules, the math required, the way the theme carries through in the directions. If you're invited to play, that's a perfect time to model your interpersonal skillls. Some kids have a hard time losing, so emphasize the joy of playing together.

P.O. BOX SCAVENGERS

Stamp collecting is part scavenger hunt, part recycling. But it's exotic to kids. Collectors use special tools. They read foreign languages that other kids can't understand. Peering through a magnifying glass and tweezing a stamp into place feels sophisticated. It's also a contemplative pastime that builds skills and expands global awareness. That's a lot of territory to cover with a square inch of paper.

GETTING SMARTER

What can your kids learn by rummaging through the mail? At a minimum, kid collectors develop their visual intelligence by scrutinizing stamps, noticing tiny details, and building visual memory. Kids use logic to sort stamps into categories, organize, compare and contrast. Beyond that, stamps stimulate curiosity and raise questions:

> *Who are those people on the stamp?*
> *Are they famous? Historic? Infamous?*
> *What's going on in the picture?*
> *Who created the image on the stamp?*

How much did the stamp cost? What's a franc?
How many alphabets are used around the world?
How do people read them?
How many ways can you say Air Mail?
Where's Liberia or Zipangu?

SCAVENGING SKILLS

Stamps are receipts that show you've paid to have your letters delivered. Like most receipts, they end up in the trash. Which means there are lots of them around, eager to be rescued. But to tap into this treasure trove, kids have to make connections. You may think stamp collecting is a solitary pursuit, but kids need a wide range of linguistic and interpersonal skills to develop their network of contributors. Here are some first steps for stamp scavengers.

1. START COLLECTING TODAY

At least once a day stamps are delivered to your house—free! Kids just need to gather them up. Put a box out and train family members to deposit used envelopes in it. If Mom or Dad works outside the home, ask if there's someone in the mail department who would be willing to collect envelopes. Have your kids write a note describing their stamp collecting project and asking for help.

2. DON'T KEEP IT A SECRET

Tell friends and relatives about the new hobby. Give them a big envelope or shoe box and ask them to tear the stamped corner off their mail or throw in the whole envelope. Pick up the donations regularly so friends don't get stuck with a pile of dusty trash. And thank them. That way they'll be motivated to keep saving.

3. INVESTIGATE

Next time you're with your relatives, have your kids ask them if they had a stamp collection when they were young. They might have an old stamp book tucked away that they'd be glad to share. That could be a real treasure for a new collector.

4. MAKE CONNECTIONS

Who else gets a lot of mail? The secretary at their school. The YMCA. The receptionist at the doctor's or dentist's office. Relatives in a retirement home might organize stamp savers there. Do you know someone who runs a business? How about a travel agent who might love to be part of their project?

5. TELL YOUR KIDS ABOUT PEN PALS IN OTHER COUNTRIES

That's the most interesting way to get foreign stamps. Another idea: Check to see if there's an embassy or consulate in your city. Kids can write about starting a stamp collection and say they'd love to have some of that country's stamps. They may get samples along with information about the country. Do you have friends or relatives who come from another land? Ask them to save envelopes and soon your kids will have a global collection.

6. PENNY-WISE PURCHASING

Some stamp and hobby stores have boxes of loose stamps for two cents apiece. Kids can spend hours selecting just a dollar's worth. Or buy "mixtures," bulk packages with hundreds of stamps to sort through. If the kids get lots of duplicates, have a trading party with friends.

7. JOIN THE CLUB

Ask around to discover other people who love stamps. Kids may find a stamp club or just a group of people who get together to talk and trade.

8. GET THE PICTURE

Collecting stamps stimulates curiosity about their origins: *What's Helvetia, anyway?* Stamp collecting is so much more fun if kids can picture the cities, landscape, and people in foreign countries. So visit a travel agency and ask for brochures on the countries whose stamps they collect. They'll get beautiful photos to paste in their albums. Then look at library books and *National Geographic* for photo-essays from around the world.

And don't forget to keep a map, atlas, or globe handy to locate the places where those stamps started their lives. It's a simple way to learn world geography.

A ROOM OF ONE'S OWN

A kid's room is headquarters for childhood. Behind the KEEP OUT sign there's a decade of carefully hoarded treasures, but to most parents the stuff looks like junk. If tidying up your kids' rooms requires a Dumpster, recruit them as interior designers.

DESIGNING IDEAS

Interior design is mental and physical work. There are three basic goals in redesigning a room:

- Create More Space

- Create the Illusion of More Space

- Make the existing space More Attractive

Before kids move the beds and boxes, they'll need to rearrange the furniture in their heads, using their visual intelligence to picture all the possibilities. Flexibility in thinking about space contributes to success in geometry, sculpture, architecture, and engineering. Once they have a plan, it's time for some math and logic—estimating, measuring, classifying, and sorting. Finally, they can apply a creative touch to make the space uniquely theirs.

A word of caution. When kids get serious about interior design, you may feel a loss of control. If you're tempted to put your two cents in, consider this: When kids organize the physical environment in which they live, they experience an increased sense of control over their emotional and mental worlds as well. That's better than a clean room.

If you're still uneasy, try to remember that interior decorating is essentially creative work, like painting. Within reason, let your kids wear the designer's hat. The plus for you? When they own the ideas, they're more likely to clean up.

CLEAR THE DECKS

- To everything there is a season. So pack away old beloved toys to free up space for new pastimes.

- Save floor space by sliding the chest of drawers into a closet. Use boxes that slide under the bed to store shoes, boots, and seasonal sports equipment.

- Hang a small hammock, basket, or net overhead for stuffed animals, toys, and sports equipment.

- Boost a low bookcase up on a sturdy table to create a study carrel.

- Shove beds against the wall to maximize floor space.

- Use furniture as barriers to create friction-free zones for siblings who share a room.

- Low bookshelves running down the middle of a table create two private study spaces. Add separate lighting, a small bulletin board, space-saving stools instead of chairs, and you've got the ingredients for peaceful cohabitation.

FLOOR TIME

Kids love to sprawl on the floor—especially under a table or desk. It's cozy. It's original. It's out of the way. Put a basket for books, a throw rug, pillows, and a flashlight under a table to create a new play space. Small carpet samples (free at many stores) can also be used to create a floor pattern, hopscotch court, or colorful pathway that can be collected up or rearranged.

OUT OF SIGHT

A good storage system is a potent weapon in the war on chaos. The first rule: Don't store junk. Donate, donate, donate!

Get a large box and label it TO GO. Toss in anything that's lost its charm—from clothes to comic books. Then help your child choose a local charity, homeless shelter, or volunteer organization that recycles household goods. Don't just drop off your donations. Take your child along to meet the people who'll benefit from their cleanup. Improve your room, improve your community. You can't teach that lesson too often.

When picking storage containers, creativity is the key. The more unusual the better. Storing socks in a mailbox appeals to kids. Try it! Here's a shortlist of possibilities: picnic basket, vegetable bin, shoe box, lunchbox, suitcase, tackle box, fishbowl, pitcher, cake pan, cigar box. Keep an eye out at thrift stores and garage and tag sales, where a small investment gets you a lot of storage.

More container ideas include:

Milk crates as modular systems
Apple baskets for books, magazines, or clothes
A pizza box under the bed for storing artwork
Jars wired together in clusters and hung by a string on the wall to hold
    pencils, marking pens, erasers, flowers
Baby carriage in a corner to hold dolls and stuffed animals

How about a junk drawer on a wall? Mount a Peg-Board over a desk. Use hooks to attach Baggies, strawberry cartons, and coffee cans. Hang up scissors, tools, and goggles. Personalize some pegs. Put your kids' pictures above hooks to snag coats, jackets, bath towels, and anything else that kids hate to hang up.

Sorting and storing belongings isn't just an exercise in tidiness. It can have a powerful effect on mental habits. It seems that organizing objects in the outer world serves as training for organizing thoughts. So when kids regularly experience organization in their physical environment, the mind mimics the bedroom. Orderliness becomes a mental as well as physical expectation.

LET THERE BE LIGHT

➺ Decorate a pull-down shade with watercolors, acrylics, or permanent marking pens. Paint a picture on a lampshade.

➺ Make frosted windows with wax paper and pressed flowers. Arrange flower petals, leaves, feathers, glitter, shavings of crayon on a piece of wax paper. Cover with a second piece of wax paper. Iron on low heat until the two papers fuse. Tape the designs into each windowpane.

➺ If you don't need curtains for privacy, string one or two clotheslines across the window and dangle objects from hooks or clothespins: a collection of stuffed animals, favorite T-shirts kids have outgrown, hats, paintings from school, postcards, birthday or baseball cards.

THE SNOOZE FESTIVAL

Beds rate right up there with food on a kid's list of favorite things. So dress 'em up. For a bedspread, just think large and colorful. Try a flag, sports banner, parachute, shawl, curtain, tablecloth, or patchwork of scarves.

Old bed-pillows become decorator items if you slip them into a bright pillowcase and sew the end shut. T-shirts or sweaters, stuffed and sewn up, make great pillows; see the section "Threadneedle Street" in chapter 7. And you can always pile a half-dozen pillows in a corner for a book nook.

FINAL TOUCHES

Kids can brighten a room with a coat of shine on secondhand items. Get an old wooden chair or stepladder and cheer it up with acrylic enamel. They'll wonder how they lived without it. Gather up some wooden picture frames at a thrift store—go for lots of shapes and sizes. Spruce them up with a coat of paint and fill them with kids' artwork or photos. Hang them in a cluster on a wall or stand them on bookshelves.

KIDS AT WORK

When kids get busy building models, painting, or doing LEGOs it's tough for them to stop. It's even tougher to clear away their projects just to make room for homework. A nice compromise is to have temporary work spaces.

TV trays are great for special projects because they can be moved around, set aside, and collapsed at the end of the project. Old trays or cookie sheets work well, too, and slip under the bed or desk with the project undisturbed.

For artists, make a large clipboard for drawing, using a piece of thick cardboard and two paper clamps. A large pizza box holds pens and pencils, while the top provides a work space. Or hang a small roll of butcher paper on the back of a door and pull down a sheet whenever inspiration strikes.

The bed is a natural work space—for kids and adults. Throw an old sheet or plastic shower curtain over it if kids are doing messy projects. Cut a piece of plywood or sturdy cardboard to fit the top of the bed. It makes a good work surface that also protects the bed from scissors and glue. Slide it behind the bed when it's not needed.

A WELL-DESERVED REST

When the pushing and painting are done, your kids may have a new environment, inside and out. When they can find their shoes, shirts, and other items most of the time, they experience a sense of security that benefits them at home, at school, and with friends. Finally, mastering the chaos gives them the feeling that all kinds of tasks can be accomplished. That kind of optimism is one of the surest indicators of mental health and successful living for children and adults.

TEN

THE EYE OF
THE BEHOLDER

Getting Smarter through Art

Visual / Spatial

Verbal / Linguistic

Musical

Kinesthetic

Logical / Mathematical

Interpersonal

Intrapersonal

NO-MESS ART

When I was about two and a half, I'd sit in my highchair long after mealtime, content to scrawl tiny lines on bits of paper. My grandmother thought my stillness was a sign of anemia and urged my mother to consult a doctor. Mums sensibly resisted and by three I'd moved on to my sister's wooden easel.

I can't recall a time when I didn't draw or paint. I still do, rarely, and instantly remember how much I love the scrape of pen on paper, the image slowly emerging from nowhere.

PICTURE THIS

You may enjoy art as much as I do, but still cringe when your kids drag out the paint. There's no doubt about it—it's messy. But so many wonderful skills are unleashed with every brush stroke that you just have to find a way to make it work. Try these ideas for a start.

NO MESS OUTDOORS

PAINTING ON THE FENCE

Painting begins as a complex process of taking a mental image or feeling and representing it in a visible form that can be shared with other people. It draws deeply on visual, kinesthetic, and intrapersonal intelligence to create and communicate ideas.

If you have good weather, help your kids set up an open-air studio. It's easy to make a hanging easel using a piece of stiff cardboard and a flat wooden hanger with a metal hook that rotates. Glue the hanger to the cardboard so that the hook sticks up over the edge of the board. Hook the easel on a fence, railing, or gate. Two clothespins will hold the paper in place. Set the cartons of paint in a bucket or shoe box so they won't tip over. Then kids can paint away with only the sidewalk running for cover. Even that can be protected with newspaper, plastic garbage bags, or an old tarp.

DISAPPEARING PAINTINGS

This is a perfect activity for kids who think they can't draw and don't want to take risks. They get to slosh watery images on the ground and watch them evaporate. Their pictures may not improve much but they will strengthen kinesthetic and visual intelligence, particularly gross motor skills.

All you need for this is a container of water and a variety of brushes. For fun, gather up toothbrushes, pastry brushes, house painting brushes, old makeup brushes, bottle brushes. Kids can paint on the sidewalk, driveway, or playground and watch their masterpieces vanish. When they're all done, empty the bucket into the garden.

CHALK

Drawing on the sidewalk with chalk is a full body experience that stimulates kinesthetic intelligence. The chalk stumbles and grinds over the rough surface, sending shock waves all the way up the arm. The dull, pedestrian walkway suddenly comes alive and there's virtually no space limit. Kids can chalk from home to the stop sign with complete abandon. Any kind of chalk will do, but you might want to look for chunky sidewalk chalk. It's easy for little kids to grip and it doesn't break. Time, rain, or a broom will erase the gallery.

NO MESS INDOORS

Part of the reason parents are reluctant to let kids paint indoors is the possibility of ending up with walls that look like Jackson Pollock was your houseguest.

ART IN A BOX

You can contain the mess by using a shallow box lid as a work space. Line it with foil or plastic bags. Lay the paper inside, put the tray or jars of paint in a shoe box alongside, and let 'em go. When the masterpiece is done, no need to pick up the paper and drip-paint the floor. Just take the whole lid and set it on the porch or on top of a cabinet until it dries.

NO-PAINT PICTURES

Lots of kids want to make art but are afraid to fail—"My paintings look stupid." Kids also go through a phase around age eight or nine when they aren't happy with their pictures unless they're realistic. They don't have to give up on themselves as artists if you introduce them to the wonderful technique of collage. Without drawing a line, kids still exercise their visual and kinesthetic intelligence by making choices and manipulating images.

What they need: a pile of old magazines, newspapers, letters, photos, cloth, colored paper, wrapping paper, bark, pressed flowers and leaves, comic books, junk mail, ribbons, box tops, labels, lace, gum wrappers, and, of course, scissors and glue.

Kids love collage because they can create almost anything they can imagine by piecing together ready-made images. It really appeals to kids with a quirky sense of humor. Using this cut-and-paste technique, they can easily create surreal, fantasy, or humorous images. Bodies with two heads, faces with three eyes, medieval creatures such as griffins and gargoyles. Collage is also a wonderful technique for scrapbook pages and handmade birthday cards.

For budding artists, you can get a free book on other art techniques by sending a self-addressed stamped envelope to:

American Crayon Company
1706 Hayes Avenue
Sandusky, OH 44870

> *As I worked diligently on my drawings, I realized that my mother's approval had come at last. No longer was I a pest or unladylike. Perhaps because there was no such thing as television and my mother could not find any-thing else for me to do, I began my career as an artist.*
>
> *Growing Up in the Sanctuary of My Imagination*
> — NICHOLASA MOHR

MORE WAYS TO HAVE LESS MESS: STORAGE

Next time you send out for a pepperoni pizza, ask if you can have an extra box. It makes a great portfolio that will hold dozens of paintings or drawings. Your young artist can collage or paint the outside, load it up, and slide it under the bed. A large gift box will work, too. Or make a large portfolio by taping two pieces of cardboard together along one side, like a big book. Tape pieces of string, yarn, or ribbon on the opposite edges, so you can tie it shut. You can slide this under a bed or stash it behind a desk

> *All art involves the physical organs—the eye and hand, the ear and voice: yet it is something more than the mere technical skill required by the organs of expression. It involves an idea, a thought, a spiritual rendering of things and yet it is other than any number of ideas by themselves. It is a living union of thought and the instrument of expression.*
>
> — JOHN DEWEY

or bookshelf. Smaller art is safe in recycled envelopes or cigar boxes.

RECOGNITION

If the gallery in your home is getting crowded, why not encourage your kids to get their art published? There's a magazine that showcases child authors and artists. To find out more, write to:

> Skipping Stones Magazine
> P.O. Box 3939
> Eugene, OR 97403-0939

Send a long self-addressed stamped envelope and ask for their guidelines and brochure.

THROUGH THE LENS

Learning to look is the real work of photography—not pushing the button. But kids can't focus on the art of the camera until you purge the urge to click. Don't try to bypass this step. Just give them an empty camera and let them "play" at taking pictures until their fingers grow weary.

GETTING AN EYEFUL

As kids practice this pantomime photography, they draw heavily on their visual and intrapersonal intelligence. The lens frames two questions: *What do I see?* and *What do I like?* Answering those two questions trains the eye to seek interesting subjects that have personal meaning.

Look at photography books together. Some excellent ones are listed at the end of this section. Talk about why some pictures look so good. Help your child notice the lighting, lines, and colors. Compare close-ups and wide-angle shots. Go through the books and put Post-its on their favorite images. Get old magazines and let your kids cut out appealing photos. Put them on the refrigerator or a bulletin board so they can start a gallery of personal favorites.

COMPOSITION

No one enjoys bad pictures—not even kids. So teach them some simple tips on composition. The most effective coaching technique is asking questions. It's almost the only way, since you can't see through the lens when they're controlling the camera, and if you grab it away, learning stops. As they look through the lens, ask:

> *Is there a lot of empty space in the picture?*
> *What's in the corners of the picture?*
> *Is the person's head right in the middle of the picture?*
> *Is there a lot of sky above it?*
> *Is there a shadow across the face?*
> *Is anyone's head cut off?*

Eventually kids internalize the questions and it shows in their pictures.

PORTRAITS

Family portraits can capture memorable moments. But too often, they're just plain boring. Teach your kids to avoid the firing squad pose. Instead, challenge them to think of new ways to arrange groups. Have people lean, squat, hold objects or pets, turn sideways, sit on a stool or bicycle, lean on a rake, look at each other instead of the camera, talk, gesture, or laugh. See if the kids can freeze-frame the action to tell a story. Making narrative photos or portraits that capture personalities is an excellent way for kids to bend their interpersonal intelligence to a creative end.

RATIONING

You may be reluctant to turn your kids loose with a camera because they can run through a roll of film faster than you can yell "Get your finger off the lens!" Snatching the camera away after their fourth sleeping-cat portrait can lead to tears. So ration. Explain that pictures cost money. Give your kids a certain number of shots and when those are used up, the camera's put away. All of a sudden shutterbugs become artists. They don't want to waste a shot and they really don't want the fun to end, so they learn to be selective.

PHOTO GIFTS

Small photo albums make wonderful gifts for relatives who live far away, especially grandparents. The next time the holidays or birthdays roll around, give kids a roll of film and ask them to create a book for the special occasion. It could have a theme like "A Day in the Life of Our Family" or just be a series of family portraits. Sequencing the pictures in an album develops logical and narrative thinking. Kids may decide to add captions or a narrative, make a title page and write a dedication.

GETTING SMARTER ABOUT PHOTOGRAPHY

There's a rich world of photo images and technical assistance waiting for you at the library.

BOOKS ON THE HISTORY OF PHOTOGRAPHY

Snowflake Bentley, by Jacqueline Martin. The biography of a self-taught scientist who photographed thousands of snowflakes.

Snapshot: America Discovers the Camera, by Kenneth Czech.

Jacques-Henri Lartigue: Boy with a Camera, by John Cech. Childhood photographs of Lartigue capturing life at the turn of the century and unique photos taken by a seven-year-old boy.

Photographers: History and Culture Through the Camera, by Nancy Jackson. Profiles the lives and work of eight American photographers.

Matthew Brady: His Life and Photographs, by George Sullivan.

BOOKS ON PHOTO TECHNIQUES

Guess Whose Shadow? by Stephen Swinburne. A photo-essay on how light creates shadow.

Shadow Play: Making Pictures with Light and Lenses, by Bernie Zubrowski. An activity book from the Boston Children's Museum.

My First Photography Book, by Dave King.

My Camera, by George Ancona. Describes the use of the 35mm camera and gives advice on lighting, composition, and action.

How to Photograph Your World, by Viki Holland.

Great Careers for People Interested in Film, Video, and Photography,
   by David Rising.

The Market Guide for Young Artists and Photographers, by Kathy
   Henderson. Lists more than one hundred markets and contests for
   people under eighteen.

Finally, to get a free booklet, "How to Make and Use a Pinhole Camera,"
kids can send fifteen cents for postage to:

Eastman Kodak Company
343 State Street
Rochester, NY 14650

LOOK BUT DON'T TOUCH

Choose the answer that best describes your attitude toward museums.

   a. Adore them! I'd sleep there if they'd let me.
   b. Once a year, whether I need it or not.
   c. Not even if you paid me!
   d. Never with children.

I'm in love with museums, but I understand parents who aren't.
They're afraid their brood will get bored, rowdy, or lost. With admission
prices approaching ten dollars a head, that's an expensive flop. Others dread

spending a precious Saturday lashed to a kid, jostled by crowds, just to catch a glimpse of a petrified beetle.

INSTITUTIONS OF HIGHER LEARNING

Despite those fears, there are lots of reasons to get thee to a gallery. For a start, most museums are multiple-intelligence smorgasbords. Kids can look, talk, touch, listen, puzzle, wonder, and even create. So it's almost never too soon for kids to meet their first museum. Here are some simple strategies to increase the odds of having a great time:

ADVANCE PLANNING

Have you ever noticed how little kids go nuts at Disneyland when Mickey Mouse appears? With all those great rides, they fall for a giant rodent. Why? Because he's familiar, 3-D, and real.

Apply that concept when planning a trip to your local museum. First, do some investigating. Find out what's in the museum and get pictures, books, or videotapes featuring a few high-interest items—shining armor, T-rex skeletons, mummified cats, or ships in bottles. If you call the museum and ask about membership, you may get a whole packet with pictures and maps. Check out the museum Web site for information on current exhibits or special events.

Now do a sneak preview with your kids. Look at the pictures and talk about your trip to the museum. When you arrive, organize your visit like a treasure hunt. Point your kids in the right direction and see if they can spot anything familiar. Kids are amazed that the tiny sculpture they saw in the book is really as big as a Buick. Savor each discovery—and then head for the exit. Resist the urge to tour the whole museum so their enthusiasm will survive for another visit.

WANDER AND WONDER

You can't plan every visit in advance. If you're in a new city or just have an hour on your hands, there are ways to have a blind date with a museum that's an affair to remember.

1. GO EARLY

Try to be there when the doors open. The galleries will be empty for a while, so kids can explore freely and you don't have to worry about losing them in a crowd.

2. CHOOSE A DIRECTION

Get a map of the museum and discuss the choices. Let your kids pick a destination and lead the way.

3. STOP AND TALK

Notice what catches their eye, then help them focus by playing visual scavenger hunt. For example, if they stop in front of a city scene, ask:

How do you think those people feel?
What are they doing?
What might you hear if you stepped inside that painting?

These simple questions develop the ability to see things from another person's point of view—the essence of interpersonal intelligence:

If they're fascinated with old tools or weapons, ask questions that probe their logical intelligence:

What do you think that's made of?
How did it work?
Who might have used it?

How heavy do you think it is?
Do people use anything like that now?

For more details, check the labels but don't insist on reading each one aloud. There's more than enough visual information to keep kids busy, especially on a first visit.

DROP-INS

Some museums are like old friends—you want lots of little visits. If your favorite museum is free or you're a member, take advantage of after-school hours when museums are deserted. Drop in for half an hour or so, but do it often. If your kids always end up at the armor exhibit, don't worry. Eventually they'll branch out, but meanwhile they're developing the museum habit.

FAMILY EVENTS

Many museums have calendars crammed with family events. Behind-the-scenes tours, hands-on science, storytelling, artmaking, and visits with experts. Some even have audio tours just for families. Don't forget to watch for seasonal events such as holiday exhibits and concerts.

DISCOVERY ROOMS

If you think museums are dull and stuffy, you're in for a surprise. Many science and natural history musuems now sport Discovery Rooms—hard-hat zones for young brains. Kinesthetic kids will be in heaven because these amazing spaces are brimming with drawers, boxes, workstations, and a platoon of helpful adults. Kids try their hand at hieroglyphics, examine shells and feathers, hold a tarantula, weave, send Morse code, classify rocks, and experiment with printmaking. It may take surgery to remove your kids (or spouse) when it's time to go home.

KNOW WHEN TO LEAVE

With acres of display cases, overstimulated kids can get museum madness and bounce from room to room, seeing nothing. Don't stay so long that your visit becomes a punishment for everyone involved. A rule of thumb: Snack, don't gorge. Then they'll be hungry for another visit.

BEFORE AND AFTER

Books are a great way to take the museum home, especially if your kids are interested in art. There are hundreds of art books that encourage linguistic and visual intelligence. Looking at all kinds of art helps kids identify their own taste. If you have young artists in your house, don't miss the excellent artists' biographies for novice readers by Ernst Raboff. Other selections include:

> *Linnea in Monet's Garden,* by Christina Bjork, in which a little girl meets the Impressionist painter Claude Monet.

> *Weekend with Picasso,* by Florian Rodari, tells how this twentieth-century giant would entertain you if you were a guest in his home.

Many fiction writers set their stories in museums. Delightful museum tales include:

> *How to Take Your Grandmother to the Museum,* by Lois Wyse and Molly Rose Goldman, in which a little girl takes her grandmother to the natural history museum.

Katie Meets the Impressionists, by James Mayhew, in which Katie climbs into five paintings and has wonderful adventures.

2095, by Jon Scieszka, in which three friends at the Museum of Natural History in New York time-travel one hundred years into the future.

The Gentleman and the Kitchen Maid, by Diane Stanley, in which two paintings fall in love.

M and M and the Mummy Mess, by Pat Ross, in which two friends steal into a new museum the week before it opens.

From the Mixed-up Files of Mrs. Basil E. Frankweiler, by E. L. Konigsburg, in which some curious kids solve a mystery in the Metropolitan Museum of Art.

If your passion is history and science, the "Eyewitness" books published by Dorling Kindersley are a museum-on-a-shelf. With dozens of titles, the series covers subjects from archaeology to volcanoes with exquisite photographs and excellent text. You can find these at the library, bookstore, or museum gift shop. They're great birthday gifts.

SECRET WORLDS

Kids live in a jumbo-size world where furniture, cars, and even eating utensils remind them that they're the small-fry. That's why dollhouses, train layouts, and tin soldiers fascinate them. Scale is turned on its head and they get to be the giants in a miniature world.

SMALL STUFF

Shrinking objects down to mini-size is more than a power game. It challenges logical and mathematical skills. To build miniature worlds, kids need to estimate, measure, and fiddle with scale and perspective, working like a set designer for Stuart Little.

Kids who enjoy constructing microworlds often have impressive intrapersonal and kinesthetic skills. They can entertain themselves for long stretches while crafting architectural or natural spaces and bringing them to life. The surprise is that they also have very refined linguistic skills, weaving elaborate stories about the heroes and villains who inhabit their world. Many times, kids will talk out loud as they play. These rambling monologues provide the freedom to experiment with story structure and create a cast of characters. Spontaneous language exercises like this help kids perform better on writing tasks at school.

SHOE BOX DIORAMAS

Shoe box dioramas capture a chunk of world, either real or imagined—a rain-forest habitat, a vacation memory, a stable for a unicorn, or the Tin Man's neighborhood.

The basic construction is easy: Sit a shoe box on its side inside its lid, making an L shape. This forms a deep window into a miniworld with a bit of a front porch.

Inside, kids can paint sky, landscape, a city scene, or an architectural interior. For a more realistic effect, cut out a background picture from a magazine, then furnish the space in the foreground to complete the picture. For example, if the background is a desert landscape, carpet the box with sand and add rocks and paper cactus of various sizes, with the larger ones in front.

SHIP IN A BOTTLE

Ships inside bottles intrigue kids. There's the how-did-they-do-that factor and the illusion of the mighty ocean captured in a jug. Kids can make their own miniature nautical world with a clear plastic juice or soda bottle.

Lay the container on its side. An adult needs to use a scissors or X-Acto knife to cut a three-sided flap in one side, like the door to a laundry chute.

Working through the chute, kids can design the interior starting with shades of blue, green, gray, and white material molded to simulate waves. Matcrials like finely shredded paper, Kleenex, tissue paper, cotton balls, cloth, paper napkins, clay, or homemade play dough create the perfect environment.

Furnish the scene with toy boats, a lighthouse, birds flying overhead, a pipe cleaner bridge like the Golden Gate, the Statue of Liberty, a wooden pier made from Popsicle sticks, matches, or twigs. This is a perfect pastime for kids with advanced kinesthetic intelligence and lots of patience. If your kids would rather sail than see a boat, turn to the section "Just Add Water" in chapter 11 for a list of boat-building books.

FISHTOWN

Kids can create a three-dimensional world for a goldfish or guppy with some old magazines and a bit of imagination. Get a bowl or aquarium with at least one flat side. Let kids browse through magazines for an interesting photo backdrop. Tape it to the flat side of the bowl with the image facing in. Then put objects inside the bowl to create a three-dimensional foreground. If the photo is a cityscape, kids can put small buildings and cars inside the bowl, creating the surreal but humorous sight of a King Kong guppy gliding down Broadway, grazing taxis and stores on its way.

211

UN-REAL ESTATE

We've all seen dollhouses that require more upkeep than a studio apartment. But kids don't need a minimansion to have fun. Making a dollhouse is as simple as rounding up some cardboard boxes and pawing through the junk drawer. Your kids don't play with dolls? How about a firehouse, train station, stable, space station, museum, or skyscraper? Ministructures are gender neutral.

To make a small starter building, get four to six sturdy shoe boxes. Stack them on their sides with all the openings facing the same way. Tape the joints between boxes with masking or packing tape. The more boxes, the higher you can go. Kids may need help with cutting doors between the rooms and holes in the ceilings for staircases. Then wrap the outside with contact paper to stabilize the whole unit and give it an attractive exterior.

The inside is a decorator's dream—all the fun and no expense. Go to a paint store with your child and beg for a book of wallpaper samples. These hefty volumes have dozens of designs, often with matching fabric. Glue the paper to the walls and use the fabric swatches for curtains, bedspreads, or rugs. While you're there, scoop up some paint chips for window shades, floor tiles, picture frames, or shingles on a roof.

Furniture can be made from matchboxes, corks, blocks, Popsicle sticks, tongue depressors, folded paper, cardboard, individual raisin boxes, thimbles, Styrofoam, wooden spools, clay, homemade play dough, bottle caps. Be sure to have scissors, tape, and glue on hand. Paste a tiny picture on a block to make a television or computer screen. Kids can make their own tiny drawings for a miniature art collection. Even easier, they'll enjoy searching for tiny pictures-within-pictures in magazines.

Kids may use miniature structures as theaters where they work on emotional problems or live out a fantasy career. This is very healthy play.

SOFT SCULPTURE

A child's brain needs a rich sensory diet to develop properly. Music, colors, tasty food, soft blankets all help the neural pathways grow. The sense of touch can be a particularly powerful tool to assist attention, memory, and learning. Unfortunately, most school-age kids are starved for tactile stimulation. That's why they drum their fingers, chew on pencils, and make spit wads. The older they get the hungrier they are.

SHAPING INTELLIGENCE

So introduce your kids to an art form that packs a tactile wallop: soft sculpture. This impromptu art form develops visual, kinesthetic, and intrapersonal intelligence almost by osmosis and the materials are cheap or free: clay, sand, dough, shaving cream, and anything else that yields to a child's hand.

Because it's so forgiving, soft sculpture is superb for kids who love to experiment. If they don't like their clay horse, they can ball him up and pinch him into a penguin. Too fat? Squeeze him until he's skinny. No mistakes. Just sensation, experimentation and fun.

The most wonderful thing about soft sculpture is that kids can actually see their ideas moving from mind to hand in an instant. They get to make dozens of choices while enjoying the deep emotional satisfaction of creating with their hands.

If you shy away from at-home art because of the mess, here are some sculpture projects that do a disappearing act when the fun is done—down the drain, down the hatch, or into the hamper. Most of these require little preparation and almost no cleanup.

A CLEAN START

Squirt shaving cream on a tray, cookie sheet, or plastic tabletop. Let kids mound and scoop, smear and smooth. When it's nice and even they can write or draw in it. This works in the bathtub, too. If the wall next to the tub is waterproof, squirt on the foam and let kids do wall drawing or practice the alphabet or spelling words. Mound the foam on the edge of the tub for sculptures.

BY THE SEA

Few kids can resist the lure of wet sand—it's so impressionable. At first they may just pound, claw, and sift through the sand, gorging on the feel of it. Then they start to build and sculpt. So if you're heading for the beach, pack up some wooden spoons, plastic cartons, a colander or sifter, paper cups, and some milk cartons. Those are the basics. Kids can explore advanced sand design if you include some texture-makers, such as a wooden meat tenderizer, a grater, ice cube tray, tea strainer, scrub brush, or cookie cutters.

But you don't have to live near the beach to give your kids a sandy treat. Dump wet sand into a plastic tub, spread it on a plastic tarp or even a cookie sheet. When kids are done, store the sand in a large plastic bag for the next time.

PEOPLE SCULPTURES

Kids can stuff their clothes with towels or newspaper to make life-size people sculptures. Add a paper bag for the head. Accessories like hats, wigs, glasses, and backpacks complete the picture. These sculptures stimulate linguistic growth when they become imaginary friends or props in a play. Try holiday figures such as a witch for the porch on Halloween.

EDIBLE SCULPTURE

Piecrust dough has a wonderful texture—soft enough to capture a perfect fingerprint yet sturdy enough to roll into worms and balls. Kids can mold it into cars, kangaroos, or carrots. Add to the fun by experimenting with food coloring. When the fun is done, sprinkle the creations with cinnamon and sugar, add a dot of butter, and bake at 350° Fahrenheit until brown on the edges. Delicious fun.

Ready-made cookie dough is another source of edible art. Give your kids a plastic knife and let them go. Their senses will get a workout as they slice, pound, roll, shape, sniff, and snack. Then bake and eat those peanut butter people and chocolate-chip pets.

HOMEMADE DOUGHS

A basic play dough recipe is 1 cup water, ½ cup flour, and 1 cup of salt cooked over low heat in a pan until rubbery and thick. Shape it by hand, roll it on a floured board, then store it in a plastic bag.

Bread dough can also be used to sculpt dozens of objects from Christmas ornaments to picture frames. Mix 4 cups of flour with 1 cup of salt. Add 1½ cups of water. Mix gently into a ball, then knead until smooth on a floured board, about five minutes. Shape into almost anything, then bake for about one hour at 325° Fahrenheit. Bread dough is easy to paint and soaks up shellac for a high shine.

CAR POOL ART

Nobody loves car pool time, but it's easier on drivers and passengers if you put kids' fingers, eyes, and imagination to work. Keep pipe cleaners and foil on hand and you'll cut squabbles and whining in half.

Multicolored pipe cleaners offer endless sculptural possibilities that nurture visual and kinesthetic intelligence. The technique is so simple. Just twist and bend. In no time kids learn how to make corners, angles, and movable joints. People, animals, and vehicles are natural subjects. Also alphabet letters, names, jewelry, and abstract designs.

Aluminum foil is another wonderful material for foolproof sculpting. Kids can scrunch and mold it into people and animals that sit, stand, or stretch. Then with another scrunch, they change position. It's easy to thicken or lengthen because the foil clings to itself.

SOFT STRUCTURES

You don't need to break out the hammers and nails for kids to play construction crew. They can design cozy private spaces or clubhouses from pillows, cushions, and linens. The following activities draw on kinesthetic and visual intelligence to help kids discover fundamental concepts about architecture and topography. They're quiet, no-cost, and provide hours of fun.

CUSHION FORTS

Let your kids collect up all the cushions in the house and make a fort, house, or cave. Kids can experiment with ideas of balance, weight, and mass to fashion doors, windows, roofs, and walls. They can cover over the top with a blanket or sheet, then crawl inside with a flashlight for reading, coloring, or secret games with dolls and toys.

PILLOW HOUSES

Collect up all the pillows in the house and make an enclosed cozy space on the bed for story time or playing with small toys.

TABLECLOTH TOWN

Spread tablecloths, towels, blankets, or sheets on the floor or bed to create a soft landscape. Mound the fabric up or stuff cloth underneath to make hills, valleys, mountains, canyons, and rivers. Create a city or village with toy cars, people, and houses. Fill jar lids with colored water to make lakes or pools.

ELEVEN

YOUR OWN
BACKYARD

Getting Smarter Out of Doors

Visual /Spatial

Verbal /Linguistic

Musical

Kinesthetic

Logical/Mathematical

Interpersonal

Intrapersonal

JUST ADD WATER

Water fascinates kids. Lakes and streams are irresistible. The simplest wading pool seems magnetic. And what kid can resist a shining puddle of rain? Whether in a bathtub or at the shore, water play expands kinesthetic, logical, and visual intelligence. With just a paper cup, a soup ladle, and a bucket, your kids can make discoveries about math and science.

LESSONS FROM THE FAUCET

For a start, water must be contained, so kids have to think about volume. While they're drowning bottles and bowls, they're wondering: *How much does this hold? How many scoops will it take to fill it? How fast will it pour out? How much more can I put in before it overflows?* They observe and adjust their actions based on the results, and that's the scientific method in action.

But there's more. As they test which objects sink and float, water sprites discover buoyancy, displacement, currents, and wave motion—all basic laws of physics. And can you think of a better way to deep-clean their fingernails?

MEASURING

A quick sweep through the kitchen cupboards and your kids are water-occupied for hours. Here's a shortlist of items that are perfect for measuring experiments:

    plastic food containers
    tea strainers
    colanders and sieves
    measuring cups and spoons
    sponges
    soup ladles
    slotted spoons
    turkey basters
    strawberry baskets

Now for a location. A bathtub is the obvious starting place, with a big towel on the floor as a splash-catcher. But if you set up on the porch or sidewalk, you don't have to worry at all. Fill a bucket, dishpan, Styrofoam ice chest, or roasting pan and turn kids loose. You'll be amazed at the number of liquid experiments they'll invent. If you decide to use a plastic wading pool, remember that kids must have supervision when they're in the water. So bring the phone out with you or just ignore it when it rings.

HOSE WRITING

While you're outside, let your kids use a garden hose as their pencil to scrawl sparkling letters across the sky. Kids who struggle with pencil and paper tasks because they're still learning to control their finger muscles can use large muscles to show off their skills. Hose writing is also excellent for kinesthetic learners who need to feel the shapes of the letters to remember them.

For a tamer version of hose writing, fill a liquid detergent bottle with water and let kids squeeze-write numbers, letters, or pictures on the sidewalk from a standing position. Again, they use large muscles and the whole body to feel, see, and remember the alphabet. Plus, there's the bonus of no messy cleanup.

SINK AND FLOAT

Scour the kitchen or bathroom for sinkers and floaters—coins, nails, screws and washers, pencils, corks, bottle caps, plastic forks and spoons, plastic toys, marbles, checkers, candles, baby bottles, combs, cartons, Popsicle sticks, and rubber bands. If your house has a junk drawer, you're set. Throw in some of those measuring objects and let kids run tests to see which ones will float.

After they've experimented for a while, encourage mathematical thinking by asking: *Is a floater always a floater? What will it take to make it sink?* Suggest that kids guess how much weight a floater can support before it goes under, then test it by piling on pebbles, pennies, or bolts.

Push their thinking on the topic of floating. Give them a ball of clay or homemade play dough to test. It will drop like a rock. Now suggest that they pinch it into a boat shape. Launch it again and let them think about what's changed.

After kids test all the objects for sink- or float-ability, pour a quarter cup of salt into a bowl of warm water and stir until the salt is dissolved. Now test the sinkers all over again. Some of them will float this time, since salt water can support heavier objects than fresh water.

BOATS OF ALL KINDS

Boat-building is a trial-and-error science that lures kids into physics, engineering, aesthetics, and lots of soggy fun. Visual, spatial, and logical intelligence are pressed into service as they observe and make mental calculations to fine-tune weight, size, and angles. Kids can spend days on test runs before organizing a neighborhood regatta.

A plastic water bottle becomes a boat in minutes. First, kids need to pour in a little water or sand for ballast and cap the bottle tightly. Then they lay it on its side, poke a hole in the top for the mast, and add paper or cloth sails.

Long skinny clown balloons are perfect flotation devices. Inflate, leaving a little tail sticking out on the end. Tie the tail and knot together to form an oval like a life buoy. With a plastic plate over the opening, kids have a catamaran. A straw in a ball of play dough makes a mast. Add a sail and hope for wind.

A block of Styrofoam makes a tough boat. Raise a mast using a pencil, pen, chopstick, straw, kitchen skewer, or plastic eating utensil. Fashion sails from paper, a handkerchief, plastic bags, or wax paper. To add a bit of fantasy, make passengers and take them on voyages.

BOOKS ABOUT BOATS

Paddle-to-the-Sea, by Holling Clancy Holling. About a toy boat's trip across the Great Lakes to the sea. A classic.

To the Island, by Charlotte Argell. Four animals go on a boating party.

Soup Ahoy! by Robert Peck. Soup and Rob get involved in a radio contest and a nautical disaster.

Boats, Boats, Boats, by Joanna Ruane. Rhyming text introduces a variety of boats.

Who Sunk the Boat?, by Pamela Allen. Animals of various sizes decide to go for a row.

If I Sailed a Boat, by Miriam Young. A boy imagines the adventures he could have in fourteen kinds of boats.

Robert Rows the River, by Carolyn Haywood. A boy finds adventure and friendship on a river near home.

The Wind in the Willows, by Kenneth Grahame. In this classic story, the river is such a central feature that it seems to be more a character than a location. Boats are both transportation and adventure vehicles for Toad and his woodland friends.

NATURE WATCH

By the age of nine, most kids can name sixteen TV shows, seven fast-food chains and just two birds. Three if you count pigeons. You can help your kids make the nature connection by learning to look and lure.

LEARNING ON THE FLY

When kids track birds over time, they extend their visual and logical intelligence. Young bird-watchers notice similarities and differences between robins and redwings. They identify seasonal patterns, such as migration and nesting. If you're lucky enough to share your neighborhood with ospreys, you can watch them spring-clean nests that are nearly a hundred years old. These observation skills transfer directly to lessons in science, math, and social studies.

BIRD FOOD

Birds aren't finicky—especially urban birds. They'll eat most seeds, including corn, sunflower, and peanuts. They won't turn their beaks up at bread crumbs, crackers, or the powdery bits at the bottom of the cereal box. In winter, slice apples into circles, run a string through the center, and hang them on a tree. If you make popcorn or cranberry chains for your Christmas tree, recycle them as bird food in January. For sticky fun, take a pinecone, smear it with peanut butter, and roll it in seeds. Hang it outside your window and spy on the snackers.

BIRD FEEDERS

There are several simple ways to make bird feeders:

→ Take a plastic milk bottle, cut a window in the side with a scissors, and fill the bottle with seeds. Tie a string through the handle to hang it.

→ Make a freestanding, portable feeder with a tin pie plate or a Frisbee. Nail it to the end of a broomstick or pole and stick it in the garden. Put birdseed in the plate and dinner is served!

→ Nail an old cookie sheet or tray onto a windowsill for close-up viewing. You might want to keep a clipboard nearby to track the birds that visit.

Just keep in mind that cats appreciate bird feeders for their own reasons, so placement is all-important. You don't want to be fattening birds for the neighborhood feline.

Bulls and hummingbirds can't resist red. If it's red sugar water, you're in for a treat as the hummers dive, then stall to guzzle down this cocktail.

Use a hamster water bottle with a spout or buy a hummer feeder. Red flowers like hibiscus will also lure hungry hummers.

BUILDING A BIRD BLIND

Once kids start feeding the birds, they should stick around to see who shows up at mealtime. A good way to observe birds without being seen is to construct a simple tent. Drive a long pole into the ground within sight of the feeders. Tape an open umbrella to the top of it. Fold a sheet in half, pin one end of it together, then drape it over the umbrella. Leave the slit open for spying. Even if the birds don't show up, this is a great retreat for reading and playing with friends. If you have binoculars, this is the time to dust them off.

FIELD GUIDES

When kids become bird-watchers, they start to ask questions. That's the time to crack open a field guide. These books are like dictionaries of birds, with information about size, colors, habitats, food, migration patterns, and songs. Field guides are plentiful and inexpensive in used book stores. Studying bird books is another way for kids to make practical use of their reading skills.

BIRDING

Tagging along with an ornithologist or amateur enthusiast is one of the easiest ways to spot elusive birds or learn to recognize birdcalls. This apprenticeship model is very effective with kids who need to move and talk while they learn. They watch the expert at work, copy, and soon become the expert in their own crowd. So join a bird-watching society or just go on a bird walk. Want to get more involved? Every year volunteers are needed to count birds on their migratory routes, especially birds on the endangered list.

COLLECTING NESTS

In autumn and winter, bare trees reveal nests of all sizes. Sometimes the wind will bring one down or you can rescue one with a bit of a climb. Birdhouses also hold little woven treasures. Kids learn a lot while deconstructing a nest. Spread a newspaper on a table or outside on the ground. Let kids gently pull the nest apart with fingers, tongs, or toothpicks. Some nests hold ribbon, yarn, thread, string, paper, newspaper, cloth, grass, leaves, and any other item that can be woven. Hummingbirds bind their tiny nests together with spiderwebs. Ask your kids to imagine building a house with their mouths to help them appreciate bird builders.

URBAN NATURE CENTERS

Beyond your own backyard, terrace, or stoop, where can you go to find nature? If there's a pond or seashore nearby, make seasonal pilgrimages. Sometimes a farm, dairy, or fish hatchery welcomes visitors for tours. Visit an arboretum, nursery, or extra-large florist for seasonal displays of flowers and foliage.

GIVING NATURE A HELPING HAND

There are hundreds of organizations dedicated to preserving the natural environment. Some take on huge issues such as global warming or the destruction of the rain forest. Others focus on neighborhood projects. Kids who join or start their own environmental groups learn to recognize the relationships among all living creatures and see the world from nature's point of view. They become analytic about problems and their solutions.

Finally, they discover ways to communicate their concerns to others. These are skills that spell success in adult life, so kids who get an early start are way ahead of the game.

If your kids have activist tendencies or discover a cause, they can make connections through city hall, the library, a community bulletin board, or your local newspaper.

⇥ If you live near the Chesapeake Bay, wetlands, or a bird refuge, you can participate in yearly migratory bird counts. Contact the Chesapeake Bay Foundation, 162 Prince George Street, Annapolis, MD 21401.

⇥ Towns along the coast have organizations such as Heal the Bay that sponsor regular beach cleanups and educational events.

⇥ Kids Against Pollution, a national organization for elementary school children, has chapters in forty-two states. Write to P.O. Box 775, Closter, NJ 07624.

⇥ Wildlife refuges often need volunteers to care for injured animals.

⇥ Tree People and similar projects work on urban reforestation. Join them for a day of tree planting.

For more information, write to:

HawkWatch International
P.O. Box 660
Salt Lake City, UT 84110

National Audubon Society
666 Pennsylvania Ave. SW, #200
Washington, DC 20003

Environment and Wildlife Protection
1725 DeSales Street NW, #500
Washington, DC 20036

National Wildlife Federation
8925 Leesburg Pike
Vienna, VA 22184

BOOKS ABOUT NATURE AND THE ENVIRONMENT

Keepers of the Earth, by Michael Caduto. This anthology combines Native American stories and environmental activities.

Where Butterflies Grow, by Joanne Ryder. Includes tips on gardens that attract butterflies.

The Wind in the Willows, by Kenneth Grahame. This classic story of Toad and his friends along the riverbank touches the heart of the natural world through its delightful stories and eloquent prose.

> *One of my earliest recollections of birding on my own was of starting out across the sagebrush desert in hot pursuit of a beautiful male oriole that flitted from bush to bush, till I ran my stubby little legs off and had to give up.*
>
> *Lifelong Boyhood:*
> *Recollections of a*
> *Naturalist Afield*
>
> — LOYE MILLER

HANGING GARDENS

Here's a paradox. People squeeze themselves into concrete-and-steel cities, then toil to re-create the countryside in window boxes, pots, and flower beds the size of a bath towel. One of the most famous urban gardeners was a king in Babylon who cultivated an artificial mound seventy feet high. His trees and meadows were irrigated with river water pumped by slaves.

Luckily, you and your kids don't have to try that hard to enjoy the company of plants. You don't even need a yard. Many apartments in Europe display small aerial gardens hanging out over the traffic. You just need a sunny spot and some imagination.

CULTIVATING INTELLIGENCE

The garden's a place to get dirty with a purpose, and even the smallest plot can yield a bumper crop of skills.

- Mathematical: counting, measuring, spacing, patterning, calculating, and the geometry of garden design

- Scientific: observing botanical processes, conducting experiments, adjusting conditions to improve growth, harvesting crops, and saving seeds for propagation

- Linguistic: reading seed packages and plant books, keeping a garden journal

- Kinesthetic: digging, pulling, squeezing, feeling the textures of soil, rocks, and seeds

Finally, young gardeners discover the deep satisfaction of working with their hands and the rewards of patience.

HOLD IT!

Almost any house or garage has dozens of containers perfect for a pot garden. Try old baskets lined with pierced plastic bags, plastic bottles with drainage holes added, coffee cans, water buckets, or Styrofoam anything.

Many containers we discard are perfect for starting seeds—egg cartons, milk cartons, fast-food containers, paper cups, and ice cream tubs.

Label the garden by spearing seed packets on chopsticks to show what's been planted where. If you have an old ruler or yardstick, jab it in the dirt so kids can monitor growth from day to day.

WHAT TO PLANT

Plant large seeds like lima beans or pumpkin seeds to fast-forward the garden cycle. Mung beans sprout quickly in a plastic bag on a damp paper towel. Use them in salads, stir-fry, or any recipe that calls for bean sprouts.

Kids can sprout seeds collected from citrus fruit, kiwi, guava, and pomegranate. A mango seed has to be sprung from its fibrous shell, but it will develop into a lovely tree if they're careful.

➥   Giant seeds that you can grow indoors include coconuts, sweet potatoes, and avocados. You can start all of these in a dish or jar of water and watch the roots develop before planting them in soil.

➥   Salad stuff grows quickly—especially radishes, carrots, and loose-leaf lettuce. Tomatoes are much slower but the taste is worth the wait.

➥   Cuttings are an easy way to start a garden and learn about plant propagation. Impatiens, pothos, ivy, and geraniums all flourish from cuttings. Stick a small piece in water or well-drained soil and let it root.

➥   Bulbs are easy to grow and wonderful to watch. "Paper-whites" and other types of narcissus, along with amaryllis, daffodils, and more are available at the nursery, in supermarkets, and through catalogs. You don't even need to put them in the ground. Just use a bowl of rocks with water or a narrow-necked vase that allows the bottom of the bulb to sit in the water while the top sprouts.

GARDEN IN A JAR

Recycle an old fishbowl or stout jar for this miniature jungle (see page 179).

SUNFLOWER FORTS AND OTHER HIDING PLACES

Here's a project for an open space, disused corner of the yard, even a patch of playground if the teacher's interested. Imagine you're planting a blueprint of a building. Plant sunflower seeds about one foot apart in a large square or rectangle. Outline the walls and leave an opening for a door. When the plants grow tall, kids will have a leafy playhouse or fort. Even when the flowers dry up and die, they'll stand in place all summer and make a special hideout.

Another green hideout is a tepee covered in vines. Stick three or four long sticks in the ground and tie their tops together to form a pyramid. Wind the string around in parallel lines from stick to stick, to form a sort of net over the structure. Plant peas, runner beans, or sweetpeas on three sides and they'll crawl up the net. In time kids will have a shady spot for reading or playing with a friend.

FIELD TRIPS

For kids who learn by looking, touching, and talking, the farmers' market is a perfect open-air classroom. They'll be fascinated by the colors, shapes, and especially the size of the fruit and vegetables grown on nearby farms. There are bulging heirloom tomatoes, parsnips crusted with dirt, and fruit for every season. Sometimes you can even buy young plants to jump-start a garden. City kids are surprised to discover that the person making change is a real live farmer who was up at the crack of dawn, harvesting produce. Encourage them to ask questions about plant life or farm life.

Visual and kinesthetic learners are intoxicated by the color, scent, and foliage of a nursery in high season. Running up and down the aisles, stepping into the dog's-breath air of a greenhouse, playing hide-and-seek among huge potted plants is like a trip to the Amazon. All the plants have Latin name tags and directions for helping them thrive, so nursery explorers can practice reading, too. You don't have to buy a thing. Just wander around and breathe deeply.

Maybe you're lucky enough to have an arboretum or botanical garden in your town. These are a gardener's paradise and a great place to pick up practical tips from experts. They often sponsor flower shows or demonstrations. You haven't lived until you've seen a dahlia the size of a dinner plate.

ONCE UPON A GARDEN

You can use your child's interest in gardening to nurture linguistic intelligence by digging into the hundreds of books inspired by the spade and sprout. Here's a sampling of what you can find at your local library. Stories are a perfect way to end a day in the garden.

Seedfolks, by Paul Fleischman.

Grandpa's Garden Lunch, by Judith Caseley.

Mrs. Rose's Garden, by Elaine Greenstein.

A Handful of Seeds, by Monica Hughes.

Daisy's Garden, by Mordicai Gerstein.

Linnea's Windowsill Garden, by Christina Bjork and Lena Anderson.

Growing Vegetable Soup, by Lois Ehlert.

Rabbit Seeds, by Bijou Le Tord.

The Secret Garden Notebook, by Judy Martin.

Where Butterflies Grow, by Joanne Ryder. Has tips on gardening to attract butterflies.

Greening the City Streets, by Barbara Huff. The story of community gardens.

Yonder, by Tony Johnson. A family plants a tree, and as the tree grows, changes, and ages, so does the family.

The Gardener, by Sarah Stewart. A child goes to live with her uncle in the city but takes her love of gardening with her.

PERMANENT PLEASURES

People press flowers and leaves for the same reason they buy picture post-cards or stoop to collect seashells. They want souvenirs of a season. Kids who press plants tend to be hyperlookers who glean their surroundings for the most perfect or unusual specimens. Shape, color, and texture are some of the criteria they use to identify potential collectibles. They're also using visual and spatial intelligence to picture three-dimensional objects flattened into two-dimensional designs.

NOVICE PRESERVATIONISTS

Although collecting may look whimsical, there's a strong undercurrent of logical intelligence running through most collectors. They have a sensitivity to patterns in the world around them that is often apparent in the way they arrange their collections. Collectors also tend to have a generous amount of intrapersonal intelligence. Independent and self-reliant, they like to spend time alone working on their collections. They know how to entertain themselves in creative ways. So teach them to preserve their memories by learning simple techniques for drying and distilling the beauty of nature.

PRESSED FLOWERS

Pressing leaves and flowers successfully depends on a simple combination of pressure and absorbency. So the next time your kids come home with a fistful of leaves or field flowers, just pull out a box of Kleenex and the phone book.

Open the book toward the back, spread out a tissue, and arrange the leaves or flowers so they're not touching each other. Cover them with another tissue and a dozen pages of the book. Repeat the process until all the specimens are pressed. Close the book and place a few books or a brick on top. Wait a day, then carefully remove the tissues. Continue pressing the leaves for two or three weeks.

Kids can leave their nature studies in the book until they're ready to use them in a project. The pages continue to absorb the water, the darkness protects the color, and the pressure preserves the shape. It's that simple. The result is a collection of papery specimens that capture memories of a season or a special place.

Suggest that kids press the leaves and stems of flowers, as well as some single petals. Rose petals are heart-shaped and make wonderful valentines when glued to colorful paper with a bit of lace or a doily.

MICRO-FAST METHOD

Autumn leaves can be dried in a microwave oven in a matter of minutes (with adult supervision). Place them between paper napkins and put them in the oven. Cover them with an upside-down coffee mug to keep the leaves from curling. Set the timer for two minutes. Remove the napkins and let the leaves cool. If they're too dry, reduce the time on the next try.

EVERLASTING ART

Once your kids master drying techniques, a whole world of arts and crafts opens up to them. With a good supply of dried flowers, some paper, and glue, they can set up a decorative arts business. Visually talented kids may spend hours sorting, categorizing, and organizing dried material. All the while they're imagining combinations and refining their designs. Handling brittle leaves and petals calls for that delicate touch that comes with kinesthetic intelligence. Some kids like to use a tweezers to coax pressed leaves into place.

Kids can exercise their interpersonal intelligence by matching the people they love with handmade gifts that capture the beauty of nature. Here are some of the gifts they can make by gluing dried flowers to plain paper items:

> stationery and envelopes
> bookmarks
> note cards
> party invitations
> wrapping paper and gift tags
> gift bags
> name cards for the dinner table
> place mats
> book covers

NATURAL LIGHT

Dried flowers make a beautiful veil to cover a simple white candle. Get small votive lights or stout candles. Brush thin white craft glue on the candle and press dried flowers and leaves into the glue. Gently brush over the flowers to preserve their color, then let the candles dry.

MIXED MEDIA

Beautiful art can be created with a combination of leaf rubbings and dried flowers. Pick fresh leaves, especially those with prominent veins or unusual shapes. Put a leaf under a piece of paper. Rub with the side of a crayon. Press hard along the veins and edges. The image can be cut out and glued to a note card or bookmark along with dried foliage and flowers.

PRESERVING IN THREE DIMENSIONS

Some flowers are too pretty or too thick to press. Kids can preserve flowers and branches in their original shapes and dimensions in several ways. Air-drying is the oldest and easiest way. Simply hang herbs, leaves, and flowers upside down in a place that is cool, dry, airy, and dark. The colors will darken but the shapes and smell are preserved so the flowers and branches can be used in dried arrangements.

Another way is to give leaves and flowers a drink of glycerin. Glycerin is an oily liquid that replaces the water in leaves so they can't dry up and crumble. You can buy glycerin at a drugstore or a floral supply store.

Cut branches from a eucalyptus or beech tree. Crush the ends of the stems with a hammer or rolling pin. This allows the liquid to be absorbed more easily. Mix a half cup of glycerin into one cup of hot water. When the liquid cools, stand the branches in it and set aside for a week or more

Winters were so long I was afraid I might forget the leaves—how big they were, what shape, what color. One summer I picked all the different kinds of leaves I could find and pressed them in a big dictionary. When winter came I took them out, so there was no chance of my forgetting.

A Grain of Wheat

— CLYDE BULLA

in a warm, dry place. Take the branches out, tie them together, and hang them upside down for a few more days. Now they're ready for arranging.

WREATHS

Making wreaths is a holiday tradition in our family. We put one on every door, inside and out. Take your kids to the woods or the flower market to get greens, eucalyptus leaves, seedpods, pinecones, acorns, berries, branches, and twigs. Start with a Styrofoam or grapevine circle. Build the wreath in layers, attaching materials with thin wire or plastic ties. Hang it from a wire or ribbon.

POTPOURRI

Some people think the nicest part of a garden is the smell, especially in the depths of winter. Kids can make easy potpourri in summer and give it away when the snow falls.

They'll need to gather flowers from the garden and gently pull the petals off. Roses and carnations are best. Try to have at least one quart of petals. Spread the petals on a screen or stretch some netting or cheesecloth over an old picture frame or cookie sheet. The idea is to let air circulate around the petals as they slowly dry (see page 177). Fresh lavender is wonderful to add to this mixture. You can grow your own or get it at the herb stand at a farmers' market. Some health stores sell dried lavender. When the petals are dry, toss with a tablespoon of orris root powder fixative.

Now the fun begins. Kids can choose from a long list of ingredients to make their own personal potpourri recipe. Encourage them to make small batches and experiment with different combinations:

strips of lemon or orange peel
dried orange or lemon slices
dried mint or sage leaves
cinnamon powder or sticks
ginger, nutmeg, allspice
pine needles

When the concoctions are perfect, seal them in a jar and let them rest for a month, shaking once in a while. Potpourri can sit in bowls to scent a room. Or cut a square of cloth, put a scoop of potpourri in the center, and tie it up with a ribbon. Tuck these pillows in drawers, shoe boxes, clothes hampers, and linen closets. A half dozen make a great gift.

HOLIDAYS PRESERVED

My family is hopelessly nostalgic about Christmas. We can't get enough of the pine-scented season, so at the end of Christmas we snip up bits of the tree and seal them in a mason jar with a card and the date. It's fun to open and inhale anytime you're in a fruitcake mood.

Here's another way to get extra mileage out of your old tree: Either decorate your discarded Christmas tree for the birds (see the section "Nature Watch" earlier in this chapter) or adopt my brother Richard's tradition. He cuts his old tree into log lengths and stores it in a box. The next year, the old tree returns as fire starter on the night we decorate the new tree. The fire positively roars up the chimney, announcing that Christmas has arrived once again.

TWELVE

THE WORLD BEYOND

Getting Smarter in

Your Community

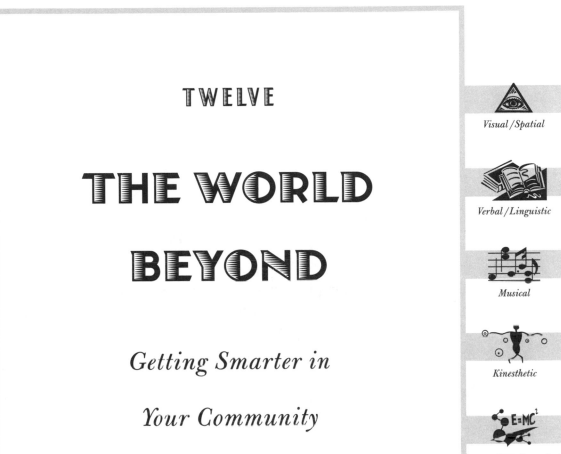

Visual /Spatial

Verbal /Linguistic

Musical

Kinesthetic

Logical/Mathematical

Interpersonal

Intrapersonal

THE BIG GIVEAWAY

There is a ten-year-old boy who builds bikes from junkers and when he's finished gives them away to homeless or sick kids. He plows most of his allowance and free time into the bicycle project.

He's just one of fourteen inspiring kids you'll meet in *It's Our World, Too! Stories of Young People Who Are Making a Difference* written by Phillip Hoose, the chronicle of ordinary kids who changed lives through their intelligence and action. Get this book! Make it bedtime reading for a week and I guarantee it will transform your kids' view of themselves in the world.

MOTIVE, MEANS, AND OPPORTUNITY

Most children are genuinely sensitive to the plight of others, and they'd pounce on the chance to be really useful. But they lack role models. Too many adults look on passively or look away when faced with problems like begging, homelessness, poverty, and discrimination. So kids feel helpless. But with a nudge in the right direction, they can go from apathetic to activist. Social action springs from a powerful combination of interpersonal and intrapersonal intelligence. Kids who are tuned in to the welfare of others learn to spot social problems, feel them from the other person's point of view, and then imagine themselves as part of the solution.

START SMALL

Even five-year-olds understand that people need a home, food, and friends. And they've probably seen enough beggars on the street to realize that some people go without. But most children don't realize that children are homeless, too. Once they know, they want to help.

So ask your kids what they could give to help less fortunate kids. They may run directly to their closet and start dragging out toys or clothes they've outgrown. Help them bag up their donations and put a big gift tag on it that says FROM _____ (their names). If they're ambivalent about parting with certain toys, don't push. Praise them for their generosity. Reinforce the importance of giving by culling your own closet for items that would be useful to others. In some families, closet-cleaning is a preholiday tradition. Children give away some of their used toys, knowing that they'll soon receive more.

Now help your kids feel their power. Look in a directory together or tell them about several places in town that could use their donations. Let them choose, then make the delivery together. When you're finished, be sure to talk about how it feels to give to others.

FEED THE HUNGRY

If you plant a summer garden, you may end up with a bumper crop and wonder how many ways you can serve zucchini before the family rebels. Pack some of that produce in a basket and go with your child to a feeding program, a shelter, or the home of an elderly neighbor.

Each time you go grocery shopping, have your child select two items for the local food bank. Put them in a special box at home and make a trip to the food bank when the box is full. Several times a year, charitable groups arrange holiday baskets for families in need. Call your local Salvation Army or feeding program and ask if your family can help stuff or deliver baskets.

When you make cookies for the holidays, have your kids bring some to your neighbors. Don't forget about your child care provider, teacher, or the school nurse. The main idea is to get your kids in the habit of thinking about others.

SHARING

Birthday parties can also be an occasion for giving. If your child has duplicate gifts, or extra balloons, candy, or prizes, suggest that they would really cheer children in a pediatric ward, shelter, or foster home.

ORDER IN THE COURT AND OTHER PUBLIC MEETINGS

When people decide to live in a community, they always make rules. No killing. No stealing. No parking from three to five. Inevitably someone breaks the rules and a justice system is required.

Children are fascinated with the what-if questions of justice. *What if you break a law but you don't know it's a law? What if our dog bites somebody while he's in the park? What if a bank robber stole some money and hid it in our backyard?* Answering these questions provides a dramatic, real-life way to develop linguistic, interpersonal, and logical intelligence. Time for a trip to court.

SEE YOU IN COURT

If you want to teach your kids about cause and effect or behavior and conse-quences, there's no better place than at the courthouse. Most trials are held behind closed doors, but the doors aren't locked. So you and your kids can eavesdrop on jury trials, civil suits, and small claims cases Monday through Friday, free and without an appointment. Head for the information desk at the courthouse. The clerk will describe the types of trials in session and point you in the right direction.

Let your kids know that they're entering a Look, Listen, and Learn zone. Go in quietly and take a seat. Don't talk during the proceedings. If you want to discuss the case, write notes back and forth or go out in the hallway.

Trials are easier for kids to follow if they recognize the players—judge, jury, attorneys, plaintiff, defendant, bailiff, court reporter. Warn them that trials last for days or weeks, so they may not hear the verdict. Afterward, ask how they think it might end.

AT CITY HALL

Kids can get a glimpse of local lawmaking and even influence the process at city council meetings. The public's welcome anytime, but try to attend when there's a kid-oriented item on the agenda—restrictions on Rollerblading, cur-few for teens, expanding soccer fields. Agendas are posted the day before at the library or outside city hall.

Kids rarely speak at public meetings, so city officials tend to sit up and take notice when a junior citizen takes the podium. If your kids decide to go public with their ideas, they'll need to fill out chits and wait to be called. After stating his or her name and address, each will have two to three min-utes of air time. School assignments in persuasive writing will take on a whole new meaning after a few trips to the podium.

COMMISSIONS

Most cities have citizen commissions that oversee business and social concerns. Here are but a few: Landmarks, Architectural Review, Tourist and Visitors, Harbor, Airport, Elderly, Women, Housing, Planning, and Zoning. These commissions usually hold monthly meetings that include a section for public input. You can follow local issues, put your two cents in, and get to know people who are making decisions that affect you. The information office at city hall has the schedule and locations of commission meetings.

Observing a citizen commission at work shows kids how people identify problems, convey information, argue, and convince.

SCHOOL BOARD MEETINGS

Most kids think that teachers run the school. A few think the principal is boss. Very few kids realize that there's a group of people in town who actually hold the reins. A visit to the local board of education meeting can be very informative. Check the agenda in advance or just drop by to see how it works. Kids perk up when they hear their school mentioned. As in other public meetings, you're welcome to share your views, even if it's just to praise your child's teacher in public.

A PUBLIC EDUCATION

There's a lot for kids to discover at city hall about democracy in action. From a front-row seat they'll observe protocol for public meetings, how to complain to city officials, how to argue without offending, being heard without raising your voice, organizing for action, and the power of one.

MEET THE PRESS

Help your kids discover the link between city hall and the press by checking for coverage of the meetings you attend. Will that building get torn down or preserved? Are Rollerblades allowed on the boardwalk? Do dogs need a leash in the parks after all? All these items usually show up in the local newspaper shortly after the meeting. Read the article aloud. Point out words that are ambiguous or reveal a bias. See if the reporter's view matches what your kids saw and heard.

LEARNING MORE ABOUT LAW

If your kids are legal eagles, introduce them to Hammurabi, a ruler in 1750 B.C. who wrote a code for living in Babylonia. His rules included:

- If a man loots while helping to put out a fire, he may be thrown into the fire.

- If a doctor makes a surgical error resulting in a patient's death, the surgeon's hand may be cut off.

- A builder who sells a poorly constructed house that collapses and kills its owner may be put to death.

Learn more about the law through history in *Justice,* by Joan Johnson, which traces the development of law in America, including First Amendment rights and due process.

IMPROVE YOURSELF, IMPROVE YOUR COMMUNITY

Childhood in America is a spectator sport. From their spot on the sidelines kids have lots of time to observe how the world works. And how it doesn't. Most kids have valuable ideas for improving their community, but nobody takes the time to ask. Worse, adults tend to dismiss kids as self-centered or unmotivated. Well, we're wrong. And by failing to involve kids in meaningful work, we squander a vast reservoir of intelligence and energy.

You may be thinking, "My kids won't even take out the trash. Why would they work for other people? For free?" Simple. Kids covet adult power and they're dying to feel important. Given a worthy cause, they'll gladly trade in the remote control for a chance to make a difference.

THE POWER OF ONE

The biggest obstacle may be finding good role models. For inspiration, introduce them to the young heroes in Phillip Hoose's book *It's Our World, Too! Stories of Young People Who Are Making a Difference.* Hoose spotlights ordinary kids who've tackled environmental hazards, homelessness, child safety, and famine. In the process they've become extraordinary.

In addition to providing the biographies, Hoose outlines ten tools for change agents, including persuasive letters and petitions, boycotts, public speaking, fund-raising, lobbying, and negotiating. It will galvanize good kids who long to leave a mark on society. And they'll be exercising their linguistic and interpersonal intelligence in arenas where it really counts. When your kids aren't devouring this book, read it yourself. It'll make you cry.

THINK GLOBALLY, ACT LOCALLY

Benjamin Franklin was a community service guru. Convinced that he helped himself by helping others, he set up the first lending library in America; gave Philadelphia paved, lighted streets and trash collection; and organized the fire brigade, police force, and free schools.

Your city probably relies on an army of volunteers, too, for everything from ticket taking to tutoring. Breaking into the circuit is as simple as calling city hall and asking for the person in charge of volunteers. If no such position exists, ask your librarian for a list of organizations in town that need help. Enterprising kids will find a wide array of opportunities where they can be useful and develop new skills. Volunteering is always a two-way exchange. Here are some ideas that can jump-start a community service project.

ANIMAL AIDES

Working with animals is an irresistible way for kids to start giving. It's particularly appealing to kids who are shy around peers or adults but have a lot of love to give four-legged creatures. Kids who are introspective, empathic, and observant can be outstanding caregivers in the animal kingdom. Check with the local zoo, wildlife rescue unit, or shelter for abandoned animals sponsored by the Society for the Prevention of Cruelty to Animals (SPCA). Most of these groups depend on volunteers for everything from feeding to leading tours. Look in the yellow pages under "Animal Shelters."

SERVING SENIORS

Most cities have programs like Meals on Wheels that provide food, care, or companionship for older citizens who live at home. There are also many seniors who live in nursing homes, far from family and friends. These homes rarely have enough paid staff or volunteers to organize card games or read to people who are visually impaired.

Some elementary school classes befriend elderly residents and make regular visits as part of their community service curriculum. After some initial shyness, young kids see beyond the wrinkles and white hair, so these visits combat ageism before it takes root. They also get a boost in their interpersonal skills as they practice the art of pleasing others. Talk to a local nursing home about their volunteer program or ask if your family can "adopt" a resident who has no visitors. You may want to drop off cookies and cards on St. Valentine's Day or bring table decorations for other holidays.

PROTECTING THE ENVIRONMENT

Caring for nature is an important value in many families. They use recycling centers, work in community gardens, support ocean projects such as Heal the Bay, campaign for wetlands preservation, or volunteer for graffiti removal. All these activities teach kids that they have the power and the responsibility to protect the environment. If you plant the seeds of social activism in young kids, the whole community will reap the harvest.

If you want to plant more trees in your town, write to the Tree People, 12601 Mulholland Drive, Beverly Hills, CA 90210, for complete information. Or write to Tree Musketeers, 406 Virginia Street, El Segundo, CA 90245, for ideas on urban reforestation.

For ocean clean-up information, write to the National Oceanic and Atmospheric Administration's Marine Debris Information Center, 312 Sutter Street, Suite 607, San Francisco, CA 94108, or 1725 DeSales Street NW, Washington, DC 20036.

For more ways to help the environment, write to the Children's Earth Fund, 40 West 20th Street, 11th Floor, New York, NY 10011.

AID FOR CHILDREN AND FAMILIES

Many children in America go to bed hungry. You can help your kids appreciate the gift of good food and regular meals by working together at a food bank. Kids are welcome to collect canned goods, sort donations, and prepare food baskets for hungry families, particularly around the holidays.

Every town has shelters where individuals or families can go in a crisis. Lots of children spend time in shelters, without the comfort of their own belongings. Have your kids donate or collect toys, art supplies, or sports equipment for kids staying at a shelter. Bake cookies and deliver them with a few coloring books, balloons, or jars of bubble juice. It would make a huge difference to kids who are feeling forlorn.

Teaching someone to read is probably the most powerful gift we can give short of organ donation. If your kids are good readers, they might join a literacy project run by the library or schools. There are after-school tutorial programs for very young children, using older children and adults as tutors.

Habitat for Humanity is a nationwide organization that builds or renovates houses for families. You and your kids can learn building skills or just help with stripping wood, painting, and sweeping up. For information write to:

Habitat for Humanity
121 Habitat Street
Americus, GA 31709

When all the volunteering and donating are done, you and your kids will find that you're the ones who came out the winners. Improve yourself, improve your community. It's a slogan that's stood the test of time.

HOMETOWN TOURIST

Do you ever wonder what tourists do when they visit your town? Having your kids research this question can lead to a year of adventures and a new appreciation for the place they call home. There's really no end to the things they can learn while wandering, looking, and talking.

WANDERING MINDS

Local explorations are an excellent way for kids to expand linguistic, spatial, interpersonal, and intrapersonal intelligence. Every outing is a chance to converse with a variety of people, ask questions, and get comfortable in new situations. They gather information that builds their store of knowledge about the world. After a few outings kids start to construct mental maps of their community, using landmarks, people, or memories to build navigation skills.

SMART STARTS

There are lots of ways to plan these mini-explorations. For a start, go to the tourist office or chamber of commerce for brochures or guidebooks. If you live in a big city, check out the travel books published by Fodor or ask your librarian for other suggestions. Read tourist information aloud with your kids and put Post-its on anything that piques their curiosity. You'll be surprised to find tours of bakeries, the newspaper, the fishmarket, a lumber mill, or the brewery just around the corner. There may be a local symphony tuning up; there may be stargazing at the college planetarium.

Develop a list of destinations and keep it handy for weekends or holidays. Before you set off, have the kids help get details about hours, tours, special events, and admission fees. Even youngsters of eight or nine can learn to get basic information by phone. They'll sharpen important linguistic skills by asking simple questions, listening closely, and making notes. And you can avoid the disappointment of arriving fifteen minutes after the last tour.

LET THEIR FINGERS DO THE WALKING

The phone book is a bonanza of tourist information. For a start, thumb to the "Museums" section. You'll be amazed at the number and novelty of the listings in your city. Museums for chocolate, clocks, firefighting, farm life, religious or ethnic groups, dolls and toys, shoes, trains, wax, seaports, skulls, medical science, local history. Some museums have a full calendar of events for families, including art making, old-time games, interviews with experts, experiments, and contests. Ask if they have a special family rate or one day a month when admission is free.

DOWN MEMORY LANE

Somewhere in town, maybe squeezed in a storefront or tucked in the basement of city hall, you have a historical society. And that's a lot more fun than it sounds. The one in my town has a stiff-spined schoolmarm who scolds naughty visitors and a Pioneers' picnic with carriage rides, antique cars, and storytellers.

Your historical society is a gateway to places that used to be and little-known local landmarks. The docents and enthusiasts who run it may lead historic homes tours or publish a brochure for self-guided adventures. Meander around town to find the original stagecoach depot or the first film studio. A closer look may uncover traces of your ancestors.

ART WALKS

Whether you live in a metropolis or a hamlet, there are sure to be some art galleries in town. Starving, sedate, or trendy, these minimuseums re-create themselves every few months with new exhibits. One month, landscape photos. The next, sculptures from wrecked cars.

Galleries celebrate their artists with public receptions. Just check the local paper for dates and times. Then slip on a comfortable pair of shoes and mingle. You can meet the artist and discuss the work with other visitors. Sign the guest book to get on the mailing list for future shows and soon your family will be regulars on the art circuit. Every visit is a chance for kids to display their visual, linguisic, and interpersonal intelligence.

You don't need a degree in art to enjoy gallery hopping, especially with kids. Their fresh eyes appreciate images that mystify adults. Ask some questions to get a conversation going:

> *What do you see?*
> *What does it remind you of?*
> *How do you think the artist made this?*
> *How would it feel to be in that painting?*
> *What sounds might you hear?*
> *What would be a good title for this sculpture?*

Other art walks might include visiting murals or a sculpture garden or wandering through an old cemetery. And don't forget about looking at architecture. Missions, cathedrals, libraries, and courthouses are all worth a visit. Take along a notebook and pause to make sketches.

SEASONAL SIGHTSEEING

Crowd watching is a loafer's sport, at its best when you're watching passionate amateurs—fly fishermen, bonsai artists, weavers, even pumpkin carvers. So keep an eye out for seasonal events that bring out dedicated hobbyists. You just show up and wander, while your kids learn old-time skills and discover a talent of their own. Watch your local newspaper for announcements about:

> Fishing derby off the pier
> Fly casting contest at the pond
> Sand castle contest
> Harvest festival
> Decorated homes tour
> Garden tour
> Dog and cat shows
> Ethnic festivals
> Model boat demonstrations
> Kite contests

In Chicago I began my practice of urban tourism, which continues to this day. I wandered everywhere, walking for hours—took buses to the end of the line, just to see where they would go—prowled around strange neighborhoods—and studied maps of the city.

Chicago Days,

Hoboken Nights

— DANIEL PINKWATER

These public events often stimulate private insights, especially for creative kids who are great observers. While watching other people at play, they may stumble upon a new interest or even glimpse an intriguing career. So pack a lunch, grab the kids, and let them discover why there's no place like home.

INDEX

A

Abracadabra Kid, The (Fleischman), 120, 159, 167

Adams, Douglas, 6

American Place Names: A Concise and Selective Dictionary for the Continental United States of America (Stewart), 95

An Actor's Life for Me (Gish), 129

Ancestor tracking, 34–40
  books on, 39–40

Angelou, Maya, 6

Animal aides, 249

Armchair traveling, 97–98

Art, 196
  books on, 208–209
  chalk drawings, 197–198
  collage, 198–199
  disappearing paintings, 197
  open-air painting, 197
  publishing, 200
  soft sculpture, 213–217
  storage, 199–200

Art galleries, 254

Audiotapes, 163–164

Autographs, 115

B

Baker, Josephine, 7, 16, 43, 47

Baker, Russell, 93

Banneker, Benjamin, 7

Bassett, Lisa, 135

Bath mitt, sewing, 140

Batter breads, 172–173

Battle, Kathleen, 6

Beadwork, 146

Beatles, the, 6

Beds, 191, 192

Bedtime journals, 22–23

Bedtime stories, 150

Beethoven, Ludwig van, 6

Bells, 44

Best Christmas Pageant Ever, The (Robinson), 129

Bicycling, with sound effects, 75

Biesty, Stephen, 57

Birds
  blinds for, 226
  collecting nests, 227
  feeders, 225–226
  field guides to, 226
  food for, 225
  watching, 224, 226–227
Biscuits, 171, 173
Blocks, 54–57
Board games, 180–183
Boats, 222–224
Book covers, 117
Boredom, 77
Bridges, 71
Browsing, in libraries, 165
Bryson, Bill, 97
Bubble making, 102–103
Building blocks, 54–57
Bulbs, 231–232
Bulla, Clyde, 120, 238

C

Caesar, Julius, 122
Calder, Alexander, 5
Calendar journals, 21
Calligraphy, 108
Cameras, 32–33
Cardboard masks, 138
Car pool art, 216
Carroll, Lewis, 16, 80, 135
Carson, Rachel, 16, 120
Carver, George Washington, 7
Cassidy, John, 103
Chalk drawings, 197–198

Chavez, Cesar, 8
Chemistry, 100–104
Chess, 183
Chicago Days, Hoboken Nights
  (Pinkwater), 48, 76, 124, 255
Choreography, 42, 43, 45
Christmas, 239
Churchill, Winston, 4
Ciphers, 122
Citizen commissions, 246
City council meetings, 245
Closet-cleaning, 243
Cocek, Christina, 109
Code writing, 121–125
  books on, 124–125
Collage, 198–199
Collections, 89–93
  books on, 92
  containers for, 91–92
  pressed flowers, 234–237
  pressed leaves, 236–238
  stamp, 184–187
Commercial board games, 183
Compass, 96
Computers, 17
Containers
  for art, 199–200
  for collections, 91–92
  for gardening, 230–231
  storage, 189–190
Conversations, 161
Cookies, 173, 178
Cooking, 170
  with bigger kids, 172–174
  books on, 174–175

with little kids, 171–172
   shows, 175–176
Courthouse, visit to, 245
Cousins, Margaret, 103
Cousteau, Jacques, 7
Criticism, 14, 78
Croquet, 73
Cryptograms, 123
Crystal gardens, 104
Cuneiform writing, 122
Cunningham, Merce, 7
Curie, Marie, 7
Cushion forts, 216
Cuttings, 231

D

Dahl, Roald, 152
Dance, 42–46
   books on, 46
Desserts, 172
Dewey, John, 200
Diaries (*see* Journals)
Dickinson, Emily, 9
Dictating, writing and, 116
Directories, old, 100
Disappearing ink, 124
Disappearing paintings, 197
Discovering (*see* Exploring and
   discovering)
Disney, Walt, 5
Dollhouses, 212
Doughs, 215
Draft animal, sewing, 143–144
Dream catchers, 22

Dress-up, 125
Dried flowers, 234–237
Driver, as imaginary occupation, 80
Dupre, Judith, 57

E

Edible gifts, 178
Edible sculpture, 214–215
Edison, Thomas, 4, 67, 100, 103
Egg salad, 174
Einstein, Albert, 4, 7, 16, 57
Empty childhood phenomenon, 15
Enchanted Places, The (Milne), 81, 114
Environmental groups and programs,
   227–228, 250–251
Erlbach, Arlene, 66
Escher, M.C., 57
Exploring and discovering
   books on, 97–98
   chemistry, 100–104
   collections, 89–93
   hometown, 252–256
   junk, 86–87
   maps, 93–97
   yellow pages, 98–100
Explosions, 102

F

Family portraits, 201
Fantasy (*see* Imaginative play)
Fast Talk, 110
Ferrell, Keith, 155
Feynman, Richard, 66, 86, 88, 148

Fictional journals, 24–25
Fiction writing, 118–120
Field guides to birds, 226
Finger-traveling, 94
Fish bowls, 211
Five-minute masks, 137
Fleischman, Sid, 120, 159, 167
Food banks, 243–244
Food section of newspaper, 159
Fragrant gifts, 176–178
Franklin, Benjamin, 6, 62, 249
Freud, Sigmund, 8
Friends, imaginary, 82

note cards, 178
photo gifts, 202
Gish, Lillian, 129
Glasses case, sewing, 143
Glove puppets, 133
Goodall, Jane, 9
Grain of Wheat, A (Bulla), 120, 238
Great Careers for People Interested in
Film, Video, and Photography
(Rising), 33
Gribbin, John, 56
Growing Up inside the Sanctuary of My
Imagination (Mohr), 10–11, 79,
154, 199

G

Gadget golf, 73
Gantos, Jack, 24
Gardening
 books on, 233–234
 containers for, 230–231
 hanging gardens, 229–230
 in a jar, 179, 232
 sunflower forts, 232
 what to plant, 231–232
Gardner, Howard, 4
Genealogy, 34–40
Gift making
 dried flowers, 236
 edible gifts, 178
 fragrant gifts, 176–178
 garden in a jar, 179
 music tapes, 179
 napkin rings, 179

H

Habitat for Humanity, 251
Haley, Alex, 6
Hall bowling, 74
Hammurabi, 247
Hanging gardens, 229–230
Heads or Tails: Stories from the Sixth
Grade (Gantos), 24
Hemingway, Ernest, 118
Henderson, Kathy, 121
Henry VIII, King of England, 123
Historical societies, 253–254
Homemade board games, 181–182
Homemade doughs, 215
Hoose, Phillip, 242, 248
Hopscotch, 75
Hose writing, 221–222
Hughes, Langston, 5, 167
Humphrey, Hubert H., 6

I

Identities, imaginary, 79–80
Imaginative play, 77–78
   books on, 83
   friends, 82
   identities, 79–80
   occupations, 80–81
   structures, 79
Interior design, 188
Interpersonal intelligence, 4, 8, 10
Intrapersonal intelligence, 4, 9, 10
Inventions, 62–67, 78, 88–89
   books on, 66–67, 88–89
Invisible ink, 124
I Spy, 109–110
It's Our World, Too! Stories of Young
   People Who Are Making a
   Difference (Hoose), 242, 248

J

Jefferson, Patsy, 106
Jefferson, Thomas, 106
Jigsaw puzzles, 147
Johnson, Joan, 247
Jordan, Barbara, 6
Jordan, Michael, 7
Journals, 20–26, 117
   bedtime, 22–23
   books on, 24–26
   calendar, 21
   dream catchers, 22
   fictional, 24–25
   jump-start, 21–22
   nonfiction, 25–26
   recipe box, 23
   vacation, 23
Jumbo puppets, 134
Junk, 86–87
Justice (Johnson), 247

K

Karaoke, 52
Kid's Address Book, The (Levine), 115
Kids' Invention Book, The (Erlbach), 66
Kindersley, Dorling, 209
Kinesthetic intelligence, 4, 7
King, Martin Luther, Jr., 8
Kwan, Michelle, 7

L

Labels, for collections, 92
Law, 247
Layered dishes, 173
Leonardo da Vinci, 14
LeShan, Eda, 83
Letters, 112–113
   books on, 113–115
Levine, Michael, 115
Libraries, 151, 164–167
Lifelong Boyhood: Recollections of a
   Naturalist Afield (Miller), 55, 229
Lighting, 191
Listening, 13–14, 160–163
Logical/mathematical intelligence, 4,
   7–8
Lyons, Mary, 128

M

Ma, Yo-Yo, 6

Macaulay, David, 57, 66, 88

Mail art, 114

Mail-order writing, 107–108

Maps, 93–97

Marathons, 76

Marceau, Marcel, 7

Marionettes, 133

Market Guide for Young Writers, The: Where and How to Sell What You Write (Henderson), 121

Masks, 136

    cardboard, 138

    five-minute, 137

    paper bag, 137–138

    paper plate, 137

    two-faced, 138

Measuring experiments, 221

Media puppets, 134

Memory books, 27–30

Memory pillow, sewing, 141

Menu planning, 159

Miller, Loye, 51, 229

Milne, Christopher, 81, 114

Mind-body connection, 42–46

Miniature golf, 73

Miniature worlds, 209

    dollhouses, 212

    fish bowls, 211

    ship in a bottle, 211

    shoe box dioramas, 210

Mitchell, Margaret, 118

Model making, 60–62

Mohr, Nicholasa, 10–11, 79, 99, 154

Monopoly, 180, 183

Multiple intelligences, theory of, 4–10

Museums, 204, 253

    advance planning and, 205

    books on, 208–209

    Discovery Rooms, 207–208

    family events, 207

    tips for visiting, 206–207

Music, 50–53, 128

Musical intelligence, 4, 6

Music tapes, for gifts, 179

N

Napkin rings, 179

National Geographic Magazine, 94–97, 187

Nature

    birds (*see* Birds)

    books on, 229

    environmental groups, 227–228

    field trips, 232–233

    gardening (*see* Gardening)

Nevelson, Louise, 5, 49

Newspapers, 156–159

Newspaper spires, 70

Newton, Isaac, 4

Nightingale, Florence, 8

Nonfiction journals, 25–26

Note cards, 178

O

Obstacle courses, 72

Occupations, imaginary, 80–81

Office worker, as imaginary occupation, 80–81
Ooblick, 103
Open-air painting, 197
Orienteering, 97
Owens, Jesse, 7

P

Painting (*see* Art)
Paper bag masks, 137–138
Paper plate masks, 137
Parker, Charlie, 6
Parks, Gordon, 16, 17
Patience, 14, 78
Patterns, 144–148
Pei, I.M., 5
Penmanship, 107
Pen pals, 112, 115, 186
People sculptures, 215
Photography
    books on, 203–204
    composition, 201
    pantomime, 200–201
    photo gifts, 202
    portraits, 201
    rationing film, 202
Pig latin, 110–111
Pillow houses, 217
Pinkwater, Daniel, 48, 76, 124, 175, 255
Playing-card columns, 69
Playwriting, 125–129
Plimpton, George, 26
Postcards, making, 114

Potpourri
    making, 238–239
    pocket, sewing, 141
Pressed flowers, 234–237
Pressed leaves, 236–238
Pretend (*see* Imaginative play)
Pulp puppets, 133–134
Puppets
    glove, 133
    jumbo, 134
    media, 134
    pulp, 133–134
    ready-made, 132–133
    spud, 133
    staging show, 135
Puzzles, 147

R

Raboff, Ernst, 208
Rampersad, Arnold, 167
Reading
    to kids, 150–151, 161–162
    libraries and, 151, 164–167
    newspapers, 156–159
    summer programs, 166–167
    tips, 151–155
Recipe box journals, 23
Returning library books, 165–166
Riddles, 111
Ringgold, Faith, 5
Rising, David, 33
Robinson, Barbara, 129
Rodia, Simon, 146

Rooms, 187–193
   beds, 191, 192
   lighting, 191
   rearranging, 188–189
   storage containers, 189–190
   work spaces, 192
Roosevelt, Eleanor, 8
Ruth, Babe, 7

S

Sand, 214
Scarf dancing, 44
School board meetings, 246
Scrambled eggs, 173
Scrap boxes, 29–30
Seeds, 231
Senior programs, 249
Sewing, 139, 191
   bath mitt, 140
   draft animal, 143–144
   glasses case, 143
   memory pillow, 141
   potpourri pocket, 141
   sleep pillow, 141–142
   sock dolls, 142
   sources of cloth, 140
   stuffed animals, 143
Shadow plays, 127
Shakespeare, William, 6, 129
Sharing, 243–244
Shaving cream, 214
Ship in a bottle, 211
Shish kebabs, 174
Shoe box dioramas, 210

Shopkeeper, as imaginary occupation, 81
Short, Will, 5
Sinatra, Frank, 6
Sinkers and floaters, 222
Skipping Stones magazine, 200
Sleep pillow, sewing, 141–142
Sling ball, 74
Smoothies, 173–174
Snack jockey, as imaginary occupation, 81
Society of Freemasons, 123
Sock dolls, 142
Soft sculpture, 213–217
   edible sculpture, 214–215
   homemade doughs, 215
   people sculptures, 215
   sand, 214
   shaving cream, 214
   soft structures, 216–217
Soft structures, 216–217
Soup, 171, 173
Soxball, 74–75
Spassky, Boris, 5
Sports, 71–72
   bicycling, with sound effects, 75
   books on, 76
   croquet, 73
   gadget golf, 73
   hall bowling, 74
   hopscotch, 75
   obstacle courses, 72
   sling ball, 74
   soxball, 74–75
   stilts, 75
   tabletop maze, 73–74

Sports section of newspaper, 158–159
Spud puppets, 133
Stamp collecting, 184–187
Stein, David, 103
Stein, Gertrude, 5
Stewart, George R., 95
Stiff Cuffs, 109
Stilts, 75
Story tapes, 162
Straw steeples, 70
Structures, imaginary, 79
Stuffed animals, sewing, 143
Styrofoam skyscrapers, 70–71
Summer reading programs, 166–167
Sunflower forts, 232
Sun tea, 172
Surely You're Joking, Mr. Feynman (Feynman), 66, 88

T

Tablecloth town, 217
Tabletop maze, 73–74
Tap dancing, 43
Tatchell, Frank, 111
Television viewing, 15, 16, 78
Theater experiences, 128–129
Thomas, Dylan, 62
Thoreau, Henry David, 9
Time machine books, 153
Toast, 171–172
Toilet paper pinnacles, 69
Tolstoy, Leo, 4
Toothpick turrets, 70

Tower building, 68
    newspaper spires, 70
    playing-card columns, 69
    straw steeples, 70
    styrofoam skyscrapers, 70–71
    toilet paper pinnacles, 69
    toothpick turrets, 70
    Tupperware towers, 69
Traveling, armchair, 97–98
Treasure maps, 96
Trials, 245
Triathlons, 76
Tubman, Harriet, 8
Tupperware towers, 69
Twain, Mark, 118
Twenty Questions, 110
Two-faced masks, 138

U

Unbelievable Bubble Book, The (Cassidy and Stein), 103
Ustinov, Peter, 82

V

Vacation journals, 23
Verbal/linguistic intelligence, 4, 5–6
Video games, 16–17
Video postcards, 30–33
Visual/spatial intelligence, 4, 5, 10
Vocabulary, 151
Voices in the Mirror (Parks), 17
Volunteering
    animal aides, 249

Volunteering *(continued)*
    environmental programs, 250–251
    family shelters, 251
    food banks, 243–244
    literacy projects, 251
    senior programs, 250

W

Wadsworth, Ginger, 120
Water play, 220
    boats, 222–224
    hose writing, 221–222
    measuring experiments, 221
    sinkers and floaters, 222
Way Things Work, The (Macaulay),
    66, 88
Weather page of newspaper, 158
Wells, H. G., 155
*What Do You Care What Other People
    Think?* (Feynman), 148
White, Michael, 56
Wilde, Oscar, 6
Wood construction, 46–49
Word games, 148
    Fast Talk, 110

I Spy, 109–110
    pig latin, 110–111
    riddles, 111
    Stiff Cuffs, 109
    Twenty Questions, 110
Workbench, 48–49
Wreaths, 238
Wright, Frank Lloyd, 16, 54
Wright, Orville, 13, 16, 86
Wright, Wilbur, 13, 16
Writing, 106
    calligraphy, 108
    code, 121–125
    dictating and, 116
    equipment for, 117
    fiction, 118–120
    letters, 112–113
    mail-order, 107–108
    pen pals, 112, 115
    playwriting, 125–129
    publishing, 120–121
    starting points for, 118

Y

Yellow pages, 98–100

About the Author

LAUREL SCHMIDT has been an educator for more than thirty years and a parent for more than twenty. In the past, she has worked as a teacher and a principal. She is currently the Student Services Administrator in Santa Monica, California, and an adjunct professor at Antioch University.